Body Stories

*Research & intimate narratives on women
transforming body image in outdoor adventure*

Edited by Lisa West-Smith, Ph.D.

To my daughters Sarah, Ariel and Adriane, and to woodswomen everywhere. May your beauty radiate from within.

BODY STORIES

Published by **adventurehaven press, edgewood, ky.**
All rights reserved.

ISBN 0-9712219-0-1

Acknowledgments

This book is the result of the combined efforts of contributors Jackie Kiewa, Nina S. Roberts, Allison Bradley, Sylvia J. Cole, T.A. Loeffler, Molly Benson Prince, Diane McManus, Ann Vilen, Jean Faulk, Mary McClintock, Donna Glee Williams, Karla Henderson and Susan Fox Rogers. My deepest thanks go to each of them. A special thanks also goes to Denise Mitten for her help during my research with *Woodswoman* trip participants; to my parents & grandparents for building our cabin and letting me play outside; to Dianna Hudak for her proofreading assistance; to Rhoda Linton, my advisor and womentor during my doctoral research on this topic at The Union Institute; to Anne LaBastille for her inspiration; and to my ever patient husband Mickey for his ongoing support.

CONTENTS

Contributors   139

INTRODUCTION

It took me a little longer than usual to get ready for this journey. I packed dusty potatoes, canned tuna, lentils, tangerines, homemade bread, sun dried tomatoes, running shoes, a handgun to comfort my husband and father, fleece duds, hiking boots, flip flops, my laptop computer and a canvas bag crammed full of the poignant stories that are the heart and soul of this book. I said, "see ya when I'm finished," as I walked out the door with too many bags in my hands.

I drove first to the bank to shuffle dollars, next to the post office to mail some after Christmas bills, then on to the supermarket to pick up some juice, milk and candies for my long overdue writing retreat. I headed south on Highway 71 through north central Kentucky as a light snow dusted our cedar spiked hills with fresh white. I was singing my most exuberant if not harmonious best with a favorite *Live* CD when I finally pulled into the gravel lane of my otherwise quiet lakeside cocoon.

The stone steps down the hill to the cabin were already covered with snow. I made a mental note to take in some firewood before it got too wet and smiled as I unlocked the three locks Dad and Gramps installed on the old wooden door years ago. The cabin smelled strongly of new pine flooring in the bunkroom we'd been working on the past two months. I unloaded the car and put away the groceries in our retro cool aqua refrigerator. I can't bear to replace it or its ancient counterpart: a matching aqua push button electric stove. They remind me of weeks spent here as a child with my beloved Grandparents. In fact, I am certain this cabin is still blessed with my Granny's kind and gentle spirit.

After a three hour-long flurry of literal and mental housekeeping, I settled myself in to begin. While fixing a cup of orange-spiced tea, I looked out at the lake as a giant sheet of ice floated by and remembered the original "body stories" that inspired this project.

They were written in the margins, over and around typed items and continued on the back pages of the questionnaire forms I used in some outdoor adventure research several years ago.

Two of my studies on the body image perceptions of active outdoorswomen directly inspired and informed this book. In an effort to measure and better understand how active outdoorswomen feel about and care for their physical selves, I collected data from 86 female respondents in a mail survey of *Woodswoman* outdoor adventure program trip participants in 1996 (West-Smith, 1997) and from 22 female participants (outdoor educators, students and wilderness guides) in 1997 in an Association for Experiential Education (AEE) Southeast Regional workshop I conducted on physical attractiveness and active outdoorswomen (West-Smith, 1997, April). Forty-seven point seven percent of the *Woodswoman* study respondents said that they had not made any attempt in the prior year to regulate their eating for weight loss, and 41% percent of the female AEE workshop participants stated that they did not make any attempt in the prior year to regulate their eating for weight loss. Forty-one percent said yes, they had, but primarily described reducing their fat intake and doing more "outdoor exercise" rather than efforts to follow any specific diet plan. An additional 18% of participants described regulating their eating to enhance their athletic performance and/or to improve their health. Given common estimates that as many as 85% of American women in the general population are on a diet at any given time, and at least 8 million females in this country alone have developed a potentially deadly eating disorder, these findings are extremely important.

Three clear themes emerged through qualitative analysis of an open-ended question: "In your mind, what do you think it takes for a woman to be physically attractive?" Rather than subscribing to media ideals of super thin, super model types, *Woodswoman* participants self-defined physical attractiveness: 1). according to a woman's perception of herself; 2). according to physical fitness; and 3). according to the body's care. A compilation definition of physical attractiveness derived from dozens of direct responses to this question is:

A woman who is physically attractive has an attitude of inner confidence that projects outwardly as beauty. This beauty is also reflected in her muscular, strong body, which is at a weight that is comfortable for her and is proportionate to her height, rather than fashion model thin. She is clean and natural looking, and her face has a pleasant expression that is attractive because it further reflects her inner confidence.

Additionally, in five point scale ratings ranging from "very unattractive" to "very attractive," 9.3% of *Woodswoman* participants said they were "unattractive"; 30.2% rated themselves as "average"; 47.7% said they were "attractive"; and 12.8% said they were "very attractive" based on their own definitions. No participants said they were "very unattractive."

While encoding this powerful data and reading so many poignant examples day after day with a gulp in my throat, it became clear to me that this anthology should be created. This book is a heartfelt collection of women's body image research findings, poetry and personal narratives that depict how their experiences as outdoorswomen have impacted their body image. It is intended to empower and inspire readers and to serve as a catalyst for further research and discourse on the potential for women and girls' body image transformation in outdoor adventure contexts. This anthology contains both compelling data and personal evidence that women who regularly participate in outdoor adventure activities such as hiking, birdwatching, camping, paddlesports, running, backpacking and rock climbing define physical attractiveness differently than do women in the general population. It includes clear examples of how we tend to reject cultural stereotypes of what is possible and appropriate for able-bodied women to physically accomplish, and thus do more, and it illustrates how our sense of being physically effective contributes positively to our sense of being physically attractive. Though we aren't totally unaffected by social pressures to meet media perpetuated stereotypes for beauty and thinness nor without risk for developing exercise compulsions or eating disorders, active outdoorswomen who take solace in nature have found, perhaps inadvertently, a way of being that affords us a positive and powerful insulation.

~~~~~~~~~~~~

As I sat in front of my computer at the cabin window, herbal tea in one hand and felt tip pen in another, I accepted that this anthology is both comprehensive and insufficient treatment of a complex topic. Although the contributors and I present a broad collection of research data and personal illustrations of body image improvement gained through regular engagement in outdoor adventure contexts and activities, much remains to be learned about why and how this happens and what the implications are for us as outdoor adventure participants and professionals.

The three chapters in this book: *Defining*, *Exploring* and *Transforming* categorize the authors' contributions from my perspective. They are compelling and invite further research and discourse. Each piece is followed by several "Questions for Reflection." These questions are offered as a starting point for personal reflection, group discussion and academic discourse that should well continue beyond the scope of any interpretation or application I may imply by asking them.

In the first section, *Defining*, authors present important research, provide relevant herstorical background, share dialogue and pose critical questions as we define some important connections between outdoor adventure and women's body image. Aussie Jackie Kiewa's research findings support my own in *Outdoor Adventure and Body Image: A Change in Focus*. Nina Roberts self-defines and places in a herstorical context a connection between climbing and body image in *From Rhythm to Rocks: An Intimate Connection*. In *A Visit with Woodswoman Anne LaBastille*, my dialogue with the Woodswoman book series author and ecologist illustrates in intimate fashion an example of self-defined physical attractiveness that is shared by many outdoorswomen. In *What Is Beauty? An Exploration of Self and Connection* Allison Bradley introduces and poses important questions on our responsibilities as educators and outdoor adventure professionals given our growing understanding of the developmental impact of outdoor adventure and experiential education programming.

In the chapter entitled *Exploring*, authors offer revealing glimpses of deeply personal outdoor adventures through which we explore our thoughts and feelings about our physical selves. In *Loyalsock Trail*, Sylvia Cole's vivid snapshot of a powerful girlhood memory illustrates the importance of role models in the context of outdoor adventure for women and girls. T.A. Loeffler explores her feelings and takes us along on her succinct *Grand Canyon Journey in Two Voices* as she constructs a symbolic bridge between place and thought with feeling. In *Shifting Desires*, Molly Benson Prince explores and perhaps cautions in a chronology of her body image development as an athlete and outdoorswoman. Marathoner Diane McManus lets us run with her in a qualifying race in *Marathon Presence* as she explores, not quite alone, the outer limits of what her body can do. Anne Vilen takes an important physical and soulful *Solo* as she reminds us of the value of and realities for women seeking solace alone in nature.

Jean Faulk opens the final section, *Transforming*, with her ethereal *Moonlight Paddle*. The contributors' passionate, lighthearted and bittersweet adventures in this chapter epitomize the potential for body image transformation through participation in outdoor activities. We travel with Mary McClintock as she kayaks for many miles in her powerful *Journey of Transformation*. In *Body*, Donna Glee Williams' voice resonates woman-power. Karla Henderson takes us *Soaring* while her students watch, and Susan Fox-Rogers' courageous *Climber Girl* eloquently punctuates our body story collection.

This anthology is offered in a spirit of hopefulness. I hope that readers will find a moment of respite from painful body stories they might know. I hope that participants, educators, clinicians, students and other professionals in experiential education and outdoor adventure contexts will take seriously the endemic proportions body image and eating disorders such as anorexia and bulimia have reached in North American and many other cultures. Chances are that half or more of the women we know are at risk if not already in trouble, and that percentage includes loved ones, peers, students, trip participants and others for and to whom we are professionally responsible. Additional research and discourse on the implications, applications and limitations of the data and personal examples contained in this anthology and other works are critical. Concepts, programs and collaborations that are emerging from the context of outdoor adventure and experiential education should be considered for their potential to effect positive change in a world where female body image and eating problems pose a serious threat to the health and well being of too many women and girls. And, of course, our personal body stories will continue to unravel.

~~~~~~~~~~~~~~~

Still curled up in my cabin chair in front of the computer, I heard a gentle scratching as the wind picked up. Ahh, the tulip poplar tree had her arms wrapped around me at the corner windows again. I got up to stretch and looked outside to discover that another morning snow had already melted into the gravel road that winds for miles around this quiet lake and cabin cocoon. The early dusk beckoned me to hurry outside.

One rabbit, a robust cat, and six white-tailed deer passed as I began a long run out past the dock. I smiled and gave thanks with my old friend, Crow. He never fails to cheer me on.

References

West-Smith, L. (1997, April). *Physical attractiveness and active outdoorswomen: Definitions, methods and research.* Symposium conducted at the Annual Southeast Regional Conference of the Association for Experiential Education, King, NC.

West-Smith, L. (1997). Body image perceptions of active outdoorswomen: Toward a new definition of physical attractiveness. *Dissertation Abstracts International.* (University Microfilms No. 9736721).

Chapter I. Defining

OUTDOOR ADVENTURE AND BODY IMAGE:
A CHANGE IN FOCUS

Jackie Kiewa

In this chapter I wish to explore mind/body integration through the concept of the "lived body." I examine the experiences and ideas of a group of women involved in outdoor activities who have found that they are, in general, satisfied with their body, and I investigate just what it is within their experience which contributes to this satisfaction.

In a society that has become obsessed with appearance, an attractive body is almost essential in the achievement of popularity and attention, particularly for young women. A woman needs to look good in order to achieve status in our society. The attractive body is made up of a number of parts, each of which should conform to some ideal. Thus hair should be shiny, and "full of body and bounce"; eyes should be large and fringed by long eyelashes; ears and nose should be small; mouth full (but not too full); breasts large but firm; waist small and tummy flat; legs long; and feet small. Skin should be satin-like and unblemished. These and other body parts have been described in such minute detail throughout the media that every woman knows how each part of her should look, and every woman knows that there are lots of bits of her that don't look as they should. Women are experts at dissecting their bodies, and are generally unhappy about what they discover (Franzoi, Kessenich and Surge, 1989). This unhappiness is fed through a large number of businesses, via the media, which capitalise on the consequent need for women to consume creams and potions, make-up and make-overs, and diet and exercise regimes.

It is difficult to maintain the body beautiful in an overwhelmingly sedentary society which produces a surplus of food. Susan Bordo (1990) has pointed out a difficult contradiction which presently exists in the Western world: in order to maintain the economy, we must consume passionately, excessively, we must become "creatures who hunger for constant and immediate satisfaction," and advertisements endeavour to sustain this consumerist approach. On the other hand, also in order to maintain this economy, we must work in order to produce, and this means self-denial and control, symbolised through the fit, muscled body.

This contradiction creates a good deal of anxiety. Generally overweight, we live in a society that adulates slimness. In sedentary jobs and always short of time, we are nevertheless pressured to turn our blob-like bodies into the lean hunting machines of our ancestors. Susan Bordo has observed that this contradiction is also denied by so much consumerist advertising that suggests that we "can have it all" - that if we simply use such and such a product, we will lose kilograms of fat quite effortlessly. The obsession with remaining slim in a generally fat society has reached the point where it has become the "central organising principle" of the lives of up to 80% of nine-year old girls in a study conducted in San Francisco (quoted in Bordo, 1989).

It would be easy to suggest that this rather obscene situation has arisen because the Western population is generally overweight. All we need to do is exercise, control our food intake, become more aware of our consumerist tendencies, and all will be fine. Not so simple. It seems that women who most fit the image of the body beautiful - those who have succeeded in the world of film, modelling, television - are no happier with their bodies than pimply, overweight teenagers. The problem is more complex than this simplified solution will allow.

I have grown up in urbanised Australia, and have, in general, been subjected to the same critical processes as other Western women. Yet, contrary to the majority of my kin (see, for example, Salem and Elovson, 1993), there have been many times when I have felt wonderfully good about myself. As I think about these times, I can recognize two major threads: one is characterized by a warm physical intimacy with my partner; the other is characterized by an afterglow of satisfaction which seems to permeate my whole being after I emerge from an absorbing and challenging activity in the outdoor environment. This afterglow is more than a feeling of achievement - it is far more than the satisfaction I have felt when I have done well academically, for example. It seems to have something to do with my total absorption in the activity, and the blend of physical and mental challenge that is typical of outdoor pursuits.

I have read a good deal of climbing literature and general philosophy about "peak experiences" and mind/body interaction, some of which has rung true for me and some of which has seemed not quite right. I decided to ask other women what was happening for them. To this end, I devised a rather complex questionnaire which incorporated both quantitative and qualitative types of questions, working on the notion that I wanted to develop an understanding of where women were at in a fairly general way, but also to provide an opportunity for women to include explanation and clarification of their responses.

My questionnaires were returned by a total of 224 women throughout Australia and New Zealand. These women were involved in a wide range of outdoor pursuits, including climbing, whitewater paddling, scuba, skiing, bushwalking or tramping, sailing, caving and cycling. Almost half of these women participated in their chosen activity more than once a week; the remainder were spread fairly evenly over the range of fortnightly, monthly, or a few times a year. Many women (sixty percent) said that they were "highly committed" to their outdoor activities, and a further twenty-five percent said that they were "fairly committed." The age range of the women was from under twenty to over sixty, although only three women were in their sixties.

I asked my respondents a number of questions, mostly relating to their body image and the influence of their participation in outdoor activities. Perhaps the most exciting thing that emerged from this study was that sixty-five percent of these women felt "satisfied," or "very satisfied" with their body. None of them felt "very dissatisfied," and only seventeen percent felt "dissatisfied." The remaining eighteen percent felt neutral, or explained that their feelings varied. Although it would have been wonderful to see one hundred percent satisfaction, when these figures are compared with the six percent satisfaction found in a 1984 study of the general population by Glamour Magazine, we can see that these women generally seem to be very different from the "norm."

So - why the difference? How have these women achieved a level of satisfaction with their body that contradicts the feelings felt by most Western women? I suspect that part of the answer lies in an unconscious change of focus. My respondents' answers to three questions highlighted this for me.

The first question asked respondents to describe what aspects of their body caused them to feel dissatisfied. Whilst twenty percent of women lamented their lack of fitness, strength, flexibility or energy, the majority of comments (sixty-three percent) related to participants' physical shape or individual body parts. For example:

The flabby bits.

My bottom and thighs - takes a lot of work to keep them in some sort of shape.

Too short; thighs unattractive; very self-conscious of upper legs; cellulite.

Being overweight. Breasts too big.

Flat chest.

This emphasis changed when women considered a second question: "What aspects of your body contribute most to feelings of satisfaction?" In answer to this, only twenty-four percent of women made any reference to body shape or appearance. Instead, seventy percent of women commented that their fitness or their competence played a major part in their feelings of body satisfaction. The following comments provide illustration:

Athletic, muscular, toned, coordinated.

I can usually rely on my body to do whatever I want it to do.

Usefulness of it!

It can meet the daily demands that I place on it.

Being capable and achieving most physical challenges I set myself.

In reflecting on the influence of their participation in outdoor activities on their body satisfaction, many of the women made further direct reference to the gratification they felt as they achieved success, overcame limitations, and performed competently. A sample of comments follow:

With satisfaction of being able to perform these activities the simpler factors of body shape seem to not be of concern.

In my twenties I agonised over my failings in the body stakes. My talent in rockclimbing made me realise that my body was strong, competent, capable, and helped me to become satisfied with my body.

I no longer feel the same pressure to conform to the popular ideal. I've always had big arms and a big torso. Now I like them.

Outdoor activity takes one's focus off oneself and onto the activity at hand.

The last comment provides, I believe, the key to the difference between these women and many other women: a change in focus. The women who participated in this project have managed to resist the pressure of the Western world that insists that appearance is everything, and we must all strive to achieve a certain kind of appearance (generally based on slimness). Although they certainly feel dissatisfied when they consider their lack of fit to the "ideal body," it seems that these women don't spend too much time engaged in this pursuit; they are far too absorbed in doing things, and are usually highly delighted with the ability of their bodies to perform.

This change in focus provides, I believe, one part of the key to body satisfaction. However, it is not the whole story. For me, a major part of my feelings of contentment lies in a feeling of total absorption in activity. At these times there is no sense of my consciousness standing "outside myself" and objectively analysing what I am doing. Rather, there is a sense of integration, of mind and body become one, a sense which can only be realized in retrospect, once I return to consciousness, much as I become aware that I have been in a deep sleep only as I awaken. And, just as the depth of sleep refreshes and rejuvenates, so the loss of ego in my "lived body" (a term used by the existentialist philosopher Sartre) exhilarates and engenders a deep sense of joy.

I wondered if other women involved in outdoor activities felt the same as I do. Complex questions about mind/body integration are difficult to pose in a mailed questionnaire, and, although my respondents expressed themselves beautifully, much has been left open and undiscussed. I cannot even be sure that the women fully understood what it was that I was trying to ask. However, responses seem to indicate that I am on the right track.

Eighty-two percent of participants in this study claimed to achieve a high or very high sense of mind/body unity whilst involved in their outdoor activity. In commenting on this phenomena, many women noted that mind/body unity tended to occur in a context of a high level of challenge matched to a high level of competence. They commented that this integration of mind and body produced the state of total absorption which was necessary in order to perform at the level required to meet these challenges. Frequently they mentioned the exhilaration and satisfaction which seems to inevitably follow such an experience, suggesting that it is the experience of mind/body unity which draws them to the activity again and again. Illustrative comments follow:

It is imperative when involved in potentially dangerous activities to have a two-way monitoring process going on between mind and body.

Best days in any outdoor activity are days where everything just flows.

You dance up cliff, execute perfect carve jike on the face of a wave, or perfect 360's as you thermal to 5000 ft. These are days you can do no wrong. Operate by feel. Mind/body are one. Utopia.

When the activity is not challenging or intense in some way full focus and unity drop to some degree.

If my mind wanders I make errors. There's no room for dreaming. Some of my best/most beautiful climbing experiences have been when it just happened - no conscious mental effort at all.

Wonderful sensation - like children - complete absorption in the moment.

One of the great lasting joys of climbing mountains or rock - is the total focus of mind/body it brings - and a detachment from mundane daily business. I think that it is this that is addictive, not the adrenaline.

Although a number of women said that the mind/body unity which they achieved through their outdoor activities could not be matched in their everyday lives, a larger proportion were able to mention many activities in which they achieved the same sense of total absorption. These activities covered a wide range of pursuits, which included a wide range of levels of stress - from lying on the beach to coping with an emergency. What these activities seem to have in common is the participant coping well with the level of stress and positively enjoying it. The activities mentioned seemed to fall into four categories, which have a good deal of overlap with each other. The first, and largest, category was that of challenge: challenging activities can involve both physical and mental challenges; they can be work or leisure related; and they can range from "coping with dangerous situations" to "fixing a bicycle." Examples included "research"; "data analysis"; "hands on therapy"; "juggling"; "karate"; and "midwifery." At the other end of this spectrum, some participants stated that they achieved a sense of mind/body unity when their bodies were relaxed and their minds were quiet. Examples included "floating in water"; "meditation"; "lying in a hot bath." A third category which has some overlap with both of these is the area of creativity and inspiration, which includes such activities as "playing and creating music"; "painting"; "writing"; "sculpting"; "viewing magnificent scenery"; and "gardening." The final category involved communicating and relationships: it included such activities as "sex/orgasm"; "intimacy"; and "talking with close friends."

Further light on the nature of this experience can be gained through an examination of the kinds of activities that engender a mind/body split. The majority of women mentioned activities that involve some degree of emotional discomfort, usually in the form of anxiety or boredom, although grief and exhaustion were also mentioned. Two major categories emerged: the first related to boredom (when engaged in repetitive or automatic activities); and the second related to high levels of stress and consequent exhaustion – which can be physical (including physical incompetence, pain and weariness), or emotional (such as crowding, overstimulation, or grief). The mind/body split was seen to be a useful strategy in the case of boredom: the mind can keep one entertained whilst the body slogs away. In the case of the second category, the stress seemed to create a situation whereby the mind lost interest in what the body was doing, or became an objective observer of the body, and this disintegration of mind and body became part of the general distress. The following quotes illustrate these phenomena:

I call it desolation: I'm going through the motions, but my subconscious mind is off somewhere else.

Sometimes with severe emotional stress the body becomes insignificant/irrelevant to life.

When I'm looking in a mirror, my mind analyses all the bits and pieces of that body - it takes a while to put myself back together again.

However, the phenomenon of mind outside body, observing the body, was seen as quite enjoyable by some respondents, who cited examples of "when drunk or stoned"; "when completely relaxed"; "during meditation"; "just before sleep" and "when near drowning." Such observations are reflective of a sense of transcendence: mind transcending the body. Whether this sense of transcendence can be reconciled with the goal of mind/body integration is not clear to me.

To summarise the above discussion: the women in this study believed that they achieved a high degree of mind/body integration through their participation in outdoor activities. In addition, a large number of them also achieved this integration in other areas of their lives, usually through engagement in challenging tasks. Whilst they also experienced times of mind/body disintegration, these phenomena frequently enabled them to deal with "mind-numbing" repetitive activities. However, a sense of splitting of mind and body was not usually seen as desirable, and, in the case of emotional stress, contributed to the sense of distress. Infrequently, women mentioned mind/body disintegration in a positive sense, in the sense of a transcendence of mind over body.

I find it particularly interesting that the desirability of this transcendence is mentioned by very few participants, especially given that historically it has been generally posited as an ideal. It is commonplace in Western society to conceive of the body and mind as separate entities. This notion has a long philosophical history, and is supported by our language and use of metaphor, which describes the mind as existing within the body, much like a person inhabiting a house. We think of the body as primarily physical, something solid and fairly robust. The mind, on the other hand, is insubstantial. We talk of telepathy and the collective unconscious, and conceive of the possibility of our mind existing unfettered by the constraints of the physical body. This idea has been very attractive to many philosophers in the past, and they have spoken of the transcendent mind as some kind of achievement. At the same time, these (male) philosophers have usually been rather derogatory about the feminine ability to reach this ideal. Apparently, whilst it is possible for men to achieve some degree of control over their bodily desires, and therefore reach great heights of knowledge and understanding, women remained trapped in their bodies through repeated pregnancies, menstruation, breast-feeding, and the general domestic chores for which they were responsible. The great philosopher still required feeding, and it was his wife who must make sure that the dinner was on the table.

Feminists have responded to this difficulty in two traditional ways. Liberal feminists have insisted that women can also be transcendent, and have focused their energies on ways to ensure that women can achieve some degree of freedom from biological and domestic demands - such as birth control, child care, and gender equity in the work place. Radical feminists, on the other hand, rather than wanting to do the male thing, have attacked the hierarchy that elevates abstract, logical reasoning over sensuous, emotional, or intuitive understanding. Radical feminists have celebrated woman's closeness to nature and her intuitive knowledge, as well as her emotional intelligence, and have insisted that this wisdom should be perceived as equal in importance to male logic.

Whilst both styles of response have made enormous strides in terms of women's equity and understanding, they both retain the division between body and mind. Yasuo Yuasa, in his book The Body: Toward an Eastern Mind-Body Theory (1987) suggests that this understanding is particularly Western in nature. Yuasa does not suggest that the distinction between mind and body does not exist in Eastern philosophy, but he suggests that the distinguishing feature of Eastern systems of thought is that mind/body unity is seen as an accomplishment.

I believe that the women in my study have discovered this "truth" for themselves. In engaging in activities which provide opportunity to experience the "lived body" they have managed to escape from the desolating experience of the transcendent consciousness, which Sartre described as a feeling that we are not full beings, a constant sense that we are "lacking," which he suggested engenders mental anguish. In addition, this sense of "living one's body" tends to prevent the objectification of ourselves, in which we look at our bodies from the point of view of the critical "Other." Existential philosophy states that such objectification of our selves leads to loss of freedom; at the very least I would suggest that it has created the opportunity for widespread dissatisfaction with our bodies.

I believe that the women in my study are, in many ways, quite exceptional. Perhaps this is to be expected, given their commitment to activities which are quite alien to many women. The women in my study are more content with their bodies than are the majority of women in our society, and they also have achieved a degree of mind/body integration that brings them a good deal of exhilaration. They have achieved this integration through their involvement in outdoor activities, but many of them also experience it in many other areas of their lives.

For those of us who are involved in the outdoors, and who work in the outdoors, these findings might confirm what we intuitively felt: that outdoor activities are a good thing! Before we rush out to recruit everyone into outdoor activities, however, I would like to mention some words of warning.

Firstly, that these women are, in general, committed. They are in the outdoors for the long term. Whether these results would also apply to people who are engaged in short term programmes is not indicated in this study.

Secondly, that the mass application of outdoor activities is bound to result in an adulteration of the pursuits. We can already see some of the side effects of this as the outdoors becomes more popular: phenomena such as increased regulations; preoccupation with equipment rather than the activity (a consumer oriented approach); and distortions of the activity to make it easy to sell (packaged and commodified "adventures" which have lost the adventure) are some of the results. In our desire to share our enthusiasm with everyone, we run the risk of destroying what we love.

Finally, I want to emphasise that, although most of the pursuits mentioned in this chapter occur in the natural environment, I have not touched on the importance of the natural environment in the lives of the women; or whether this environment plays a crucial part in the achievement of the benefits mentioned in this chapter; nor have I mentioned any degradation of the environment which may be resulting from their activities. Once again, these aspects need to be addressed.

References

Bordo, S. (1990). Reading the slender body. In M. Jacobus, E.F. Keller, & S. Shuttleworth (Eds.) *Body politics: Women and the discourses of science.* New York: Routledge.

Bordo, S. (1989). The body and the reproduction of femininity: A feminist appropriation of Foucalt. In A.M. Jaggar & S. R. Bordo (Eds.) *Gender/Body/Knowledge: Feminist reconstructions of being and knowing.* New Brunswick: Rutgers University Press.

Franzoi, S.L., Kessenich, J.J. & Surge, P.A. (1989). Gender differences in the experience of body awareness: An experiential sampling study, *Sex Roles, 21* (7/8), 499-515.

Salem, S.K. & Elovson, A.C. (1993). *Importance of ideal body image, self esteem and depression in females.* Paper presented at the Annual Convention of the American Psychological Association.

Sartre, Jean-Paul (1997). H. E. Barnes (Trans.) *Being and nothingness: An essay in phenomenological ontology.* Secaucus, New Jersey: The Citadel Press. (Original work published 1956)

Yuasa, Y. (1987). *The body: Toward an Eastern mind-body theory.* New York: State University of New York Press.

Questions for Reflection

1. What actions, if any, do you feel should be taken by outdoor adventure professionals given this and other authors' estimates of higher body image satisfaction among women who are active in outdoor adventure than those in the general population?

2. How do these findings compare with your own experience?

3. What role do you believe outdoor adventure education should play in the field of body image and eating disorder prevention and intervention?

FROM RHYTHM TO ROCKS: AN INTIMATE CONNECTION

Nina S. Roberts

We must all see ourselves as part of nature. ~ Navajo Nation

Rock climbing is an activity that gives room for individual character and fire and passion. The wild sweet moments on any given route, the extremes of tension and peace, don't seem to happen to me during other outdoor activities. Like exploration, I believe the charm of climbing is in self-knowledge derived from personal interaction with natural forces. When I am on the rocks, I see myself "as part of nature," fully and completely.

I understand my body as not being separate from the land, or from the rocks. My feet are made to keep me grounded, my body a vessel to carry me forward. As a woman, I believe the female body is an instrument of knowing. To take much pleasure in the natural world, filled with so much beauty, is a joy in life that all women should experience. Each woman has her own ways of knowing and being, just as there are many kinds of bird in flight, many species of pine trees, and a variety of beautiful fish swimming in the river.

When I'm climbing on rocks whether free climbing or on belay, I feel like a dancer, an artist, applying agility and finesse to work out delicate cruxes and moving beyond tenuous stances and holds. Rock climbing is a meaningful part of life that gives me access to parts of my body and mind that are usually inaccessible. For example, when I am climbing, I uncover incredibly deep feelings of personal understanding about myself that I never knew existed. Climbing gives me a great amount of pride, teaches me what I can do; it teaches me honesty and open-mindedness.

For me, climbing is a celebration of the spirit in a way that feels like I'm "home." And, I've learned about both the power and nourishment from those women who have climbed before me.

The Early Fight for Equality and Freedom

Through literature review and personal research, I've learned that the story of women in climbing (and mountaineering) goes back a couple of hundred years. In their book, "Women Climbing: 200 Years of Achievement," Birkett and Peascod (1989) have given us an extraordinary collection of female pioneers around the world who, against extreme social pressures and adversity, have tremendous journeys of success and endeavor. For instance, we learned that women climbers in the early 19th century treaded on male egos. And, in opposition to traditional gender roles, they dared to wear trousers on the hills and step into the natural world at a time when society regarded the women's place to be in the home.

From the beginning of the 1800s, women climbed with a sense of guilt. They climbed even when suppressed; they were ignored, then gradually accepted with reluctance, but only as something less than serious (Birkett & Peascod, 1989). Although it has taken several decades, we have entered an era where few can doubt the achievements of women, or question our abilities and potential.

Despite much progress, throughout the early literature we see testimony of women's physical inferiority and skepticism of women's mental ability to endure. While there are many instances where this is known to be truth, one illustration of this is when our male allies ask "how can a woman, a mere girl, so obviously feminine, climb that hard?" (Birkett & Peascod, 1989, 11). I've also seen women's abilities to perform on the rocks questioned first-hand through my involvement with women in the outdoors in varying capacities for over fifteen years. As a participant, instructor, researcher, trainer, and mentor for others, I've encountered both captivating stories and detail from data collected in empirical studies across the country that support this.

Success at rock climbing, for instance, is perceived by both women and men to require tremendous amounts of muscular strength (Roberts, 1992; Roberts, 1997). For many women, this perception has historically been, and in many instances still is, a significant barrier that discourages their attempts at climbing. During my graduate studies. I completed my thesis research on the contents of *Climbing* magazine over a twenty-year period. In this study, the question of muscular strength surfaced numerous times. Specifically, I wanted to know how women climbers were portrayed. The study contained 2,206 direct references to male climbers and 276 mentions of female climbers, a ratio of 8 to 1. While results indicate there was an increase in the proportional amount of coverage given to females (primarily in the 1980s), there was also an inspirational shift in the emphasis given to females from passive observers to active climbers, strong women and expedition leaders (Roberts, 1992).

This study also revealed that a lack of self-assurance and confidence in potential ability is a known constraint for many women; this makes it difficult to test personal limits and explore the capabilities of one's body. Secondly, because it has taken female climbers several decades to surpass the negative stereotype that such activities are believed to be "unfeminine," many of those women who did participate in the early years were devalued. Consequently, with increased acceptance and skill development, more women are climbing at higher standards than ever before. And, we have gained respect and recognition that is sharper now as at any point in history.

A personal example is when I was teaching a beginning rock climbing class. I was leading a group of novice women on a relatively "easy" climb; there was a group of young men top roping on an ascent next to our climbing site. I over heard one fellow say to his friend: " These girls don't have a chance on that route, it's way too hard for them." My heart sank. First, I felt my instruction was being questioned by someone who didn't even know me, and second, this group of women (not "girls") was being hindered by assumptions. Furthermore, returning to the literature, one article that I read in *Climbing* magazine stands out. Mimi Stone spoke about practicing one day and noted that a little girl came running over to the rock that she was on and started climbing it. She mentioned she was right near the little girl. Her mother apparently came over and towed her away, telling her that girls didn't do that kind of thing. And, Mimi was right there! She mentioned that she'd like to get to the top of Everest because she'd like to do it, but that she's also out there climbing so that little girls like that one know that we *do* do that (Roberts, 1992).

Another example found in the literature is from a study conducted in 1987. Researchers compared and contrasted female and male rock climbers in terms of skill level, experience, number of participants and social contexts of participation. They concluded that climbing was perceived as too difficult for women. However, results also show the expertise and experience women demonstrate in rock climbing is "equal to that of men." Based on the data they collected, it appeared that the main barrier to participation is not skill and ability, but rather cultural stereotypes and misconceptions regarding whether rock climbing is an appropriate leisure activity for women (Hollenhorst, 1988).

The Hollenhorst study included remarks on the fact that biological differences clearly exist between men and women, and it is the muscular strength that can be distinguished by physiological make up of the body. While this may be accurate, we have learned that, on many occasions, the physical and mental difficulties of the act of climbing have proved secondary to the prejudices and problems imposed by society. Although there has been little documentation, an integrative review of the literature confirms that skills and ability are not necessarily limitations for women as much as cultural stereotypes and misconceptions (Henderson & Roberts, 1998).

A Journey of Excitement and Wonder

The Early Years

My first exposure to rock climbing came from hearing the stories told by my older sister each time she returned from her climbing trips. Her involvement and experiences in the late 70's, (as with many women during this time) occurred with her boyfriend. Although she would brag about how much fun it was and encourage me to try, I rarely had any interest. My activities during these high school years took place on the basketball court and lacrosse field. To my astonishment, she came home one day with an injury that caused pain and scarring for weeks. A massive rope burn down the entire length of her back sent the message to me that climbing was "dangerous" and perhaps not that much fun or worth trying after all!

Half way up the rocks, my sister noted going "beyond her ability." She panicked. Entering a state of fear and uncertainty in what her mind and body could handle, she told her boyfriend she was coming down. Her shirt came untucked and, subsequently her level of fear heightened. As she was afraid to let go to tuck in her shirt, the rope got caught between the skin of her back and clothing that may have provided a bit of protection. Her frustration upon returning to the ground was accentuated with a lengthy abrasion that became part of her world for quite a while following this event. This impacted her experience, and learning of her adventures both excited and scared me. As a result, I became more interested to learn how rock climbing might teach me more about my body and the connection to both my feelings and intellect. My body is multifaceted and craves protection. It speaks through its color and its temperature; it speaks through the dynamic movements, the glow of love, the remnants of pain, and the heat of arousal. And, it speaks through dance, sometimes swaying with a magical rhythm, sometimes it trembles with reservation. I take risks with my body to learn what it can do, yet I dance around the fear of possible injury. Learning to accept this fear, to take it in without letting it take over is one of the challenges I've always embraced through sports. By taking risks with my body, knowing injury may occur, I sharpen my senses.

Through years of experience with athletics and weight training, my body remembers its evolution; my bones remember, as do my joints, as they endured the many sprains and strains I encountered from playing hard. Even my fingers remember! And, memories of my fingers from my first day on the rocks are vivid. As many friends and co-workers of mine began to rock climb, the encouragement for me to try came on even stronger.   One weekend on a warm spring day, a few of my colleagues were heading to the Quincy Quarries (outside of Boston) and invited me to come along.

I was uncomfortable with the conquering quality that seemed so pronounced with this activity. Hesitantly, I joined the group - five men and me. Perhaps the instruction I received was less than competent, but aside from the sheer beauty of the Quarries, I remember nothing but the miserable pain in my fingers trying to grip the rock on various pencil thin handholds. I was not afraid of injury, nor of falling. I learned to welcome being on the edge; I welcomed the adrenaline rush through my body. Nonetheless, I found little pleasure in aching fingers. Continuously I'd meet more and more climbers, both women and men, who convinced me that rock climbing could, in fact, provide me with that mental and physical exhilaration that I seek in much of my personal recreation. Somehow I knew there was truth to this. Hiking through the forests and parks, I'd observe people experiencing the flow and challenge of ascending the naturalness of the earth's solid rocks. My curiosity and wonder continued to rise.

A parallel that can be made here relates to dancing as a metaphor. The rhythm I have on the dance floor is smooth and physically energizing. I believed that with proper training and opportunity, my body could move with the same rhythm on the rocks. And, I knew I was strong enough to handle it as well. We are all blessed with two kinds of strength: the strength of muscles and the strength of soul. I've learned to listen to my body and to provide it with varying activities that will sculpt it and connect it to the natural world. I became determined to master the skills of rock climbing.

Learning, Teaching, Experiencing

During the early 80's, I sought to receive training from a variety of outstanding instructors, both women and men. I learned the language, the moves and myriad of body positions. I learned to talk to the rocks, to the wild and silent world we often take for granted. I learned how to breathe, to generate my own flow, to create my own batch of courage.

Nina Roberts rock dancing

Over time, I acquired the necessary training and experience, and began teaching these technical skills to both youth and adults. Resulting from additional education and training, and more personal climbing experience, I moved beyond mere technical skill development. That is, I would never lead a group without building in the value and significance of learning to "dance" on the rocks. The participants in my programs are encouraged to nourish their bodies as much as possible in order to stay healthy and strong. They are encouraged to accept their own body and listen to their body as a powerful being.

As both a participant and guide of all-women's groups, I've always enjoyed the incredible camaraderie and feeling of freedom. My style of leading grew to integrate technical skills and safety techniques, with total body awareness and attention given to the richness of the female mind to maintain control over one's self.

I share the conviction with many of my female comadres that women ought to experience movement of their bodies in a way they may never think is possible. Women in my groups are encouraged to use their intuition, and to experiment with the smooth yet complex movements of their bodies as they connect with the intricacies of the rock. I encourage women to perfect their movements in order to learn more about themselves. Grace, flexibility, balance, power, relaxation, strength, judgment, and self-confidence; these are the ingredients for experiencing movement on the rocks with precision and creativity.

For me, climbing is powerful movement, a rhythmic dance, a soft whisper, and exerting triumph all mixed together. When I climb, my body rocks, my mind soars, and I establish an intimate connection with the natural environment. There's a tremendous range of feelings I endure when I'm at a significant distance above the ground. A tingling, forceful flow of blood rushes through my legs, my arms, my torso. My mind experiences a solid, spiritual connection to my surroundings; the rhythm takes hold, and the dance begins again.

The Challenge Continues

From climbing rocks in the Quincy Quarries to climbing ice in the White Mountains, I've gained a variety of skills over the years. I've enjoyed opportunities in Wisconsin and Minnesota with Woodswomen as well as experiences on the spectacular cliffs in southeastern Arizona with the National Outdoor Leadership School to learn varying philosophies. Although I can't say I have done Devil's Tower or El Capitan, or even climbed internationally, I can say that my journey has been fulfilling and powerful.

In her book, "Leading out: Women climbers reaching for the top," Rachel da Silva made an outstanding contribution to the world of women climbers by compiling an awesome collection of women's writing on climbing. The exceptional growth of women's participation is well reflected in this collection. In her introduction, Rachel notes climbing has been pulled and shaped by new forces in several different directions. She reminds us of the deep thoughtful analysis of what many women go through in pursuit of their dreams.

The challenge to elevate my own standards and abilities continues. More than anything else, climbing is a reliance upon and understanding of my innermost being. While I feel like I've reached a plateau in my climbing, I continue to draw from my past experiences and use my tenacious desire to learn and improve. And, deep inside my soul lies the road to follow, not my destiny. The expectation I have of myself is what continuously motivates me on to the next challenge. Throughout my journey, because I'm willing to risk failure, I know I'll succeed a lot more.

Acknowledgments: I would like to thank Dr. Rita Yerkes, Dean of George Williams College at Aurora University, for her encouraging and astute review of this chapter. She's been a mentor and friend for many years and has provided important insight and feedback for completion of this paper. Thanks also to Lisa West-Smith for her very valuable comments in bringing this work to fruition, and for following her dreams and vision for creation of this book in general.

References

Birkett, B. & Peascod, B. (1989). *Women climbing: 200 years of achievement.* Seattle, WA: The Mountaineers.

daSilva, R. (1992). *Leading out: Women climbers reaching for the top.* Seattle, WA: Seal Press.

Henderson, K.A. & Roberts, N.S. (1998, January). *An integrative review of the literature on women in the outdoors.* Paper presented to the 4th Biennial Coalition for Education in the Outdoors Research Symposium, Bradford Woods, Martinsville, IN.

Hollenhorst, S. (1988). Rock climbers. *Women in Natural Resources, 10*(2), 15-36.

Roberts, N.S. (Ed.). (1997). *A guide to women's studies in the outdoors: A review of literature and research with annotated bibliography.* Needham Heights, MA: Simon & Schuster Custom Publishing.

Roberts, N.S. (1992). Portrayal of women in Climbing magazine, A content analysis: 1970-1990. *Master's Abstracts International.* (University Microfilms No. MA0043100001).

Questions for Reflection

1. What do you think about cultural expectations or norms for what women and girls are expected to be strong enough to accomplish?

2. How do you think that climbing has impacted this author's expectations for herself in other life areas- personally and professionally?

3. How has your own experience in an outdoor activity- like climbing, or paddling or hiking- impacted your expectations of what you can accomplish in other areas of your life?

A VISIT WITH WOODSWOMAN ANNE LABASTILLE

Lisa West-Smith

"May I have your sex?" I could have sworn I heard the woman say.

"WHAT?" I replied, ever so rudely.

"May I have your sex?" the caller repeated patiently. By this time, I was openly hostile.

"WHO IS THIS?" I demanded angrily. I mean geez, it was 7:40 AM, and I was completed lost in some tedious record keeping.

The caller articulated clearly and still patiently though slightly louder this time, "This is Dr. LaBastille calling from New York. May I have your fax please?"

Whoops. Thus began the first conversation I ever had with Dr. Anne LaBastille.

Wildlife ecologist, conservationist, author and wilderness guide Anne LaBastille, Ph.D. is probably best known and admired by fans like me for her *Woodswoman* book series. In the *Woodswoman* trilogy, Anne describes in compelling detail her struggles and triumphs from the cabin she built in the Adirondack Park area of upstate New York. Thousands of her readers have been and continue to be inspired by her personal and professional tenacity, courage, passion and commitment to wild creatures and protection of the natural spaces they inhabit.

I was aware as I rolled down the window in my tiny red rental car that many people would gladly have traded jobs with me this week. I was nervously eager for this trip, even more so since my humorous beginning with Anne. The fax she was trying to send me that late summer morning was in response to my request to interview her for this anthology. Anne was in the process of preparing her recently acquired old farmstead for the winter. I would have to meet with her there, rather than at the cabin, she told me as we laughed over my mistake. Of course a farm visit with Anne LaBastille was just fine with me. With my modest canoeing skills, I was worried about not being able to keep up with her on a paddling journey to the remote cabin; it is located two miles from the nearest dirt road on the edge of a huge wilderness tract and stands solidly without electricity or indoor plumbing. I worked hard to maintain my cool as we chose dates and I got the directions from the airport to her farm at the edge of the Adirondack Park. You have to remember you are a professional, I thought to myself many times during this process. You can't be a gushing fan and her guest for three days and expect to conduct a reasonable interview. So I drive on, passing Lake George and the High Peaks, taking pictures out of the window of my car like an idiot.

Just as Anne warned, I had to slow down on the long final road to her white farm house to make way for a large, loud and ferocious looking German Shepherd escort up the driveway. Xandor inspected me carefully and quickly; I must have passed. He gave me a good wagging tail smack and an affectionate lick to my upturned palm, and ran off to tell Anne his new friend was here.

Anne was everything and nothing like I expected. She padded down the steps of the side porch, barefooted with pink toenails to match pink lipstick, wearing a warm smile.

"Lisa?" she said, grasping my hand for a firm shake. Her long silver-blonde hair contrasted starkly with her black jeans and T-shirt, and her lean silhouette belied the strength of her sinewy frame.

"Yes, and you must be Anne," I said happily, so excited to meet the woman who had inspired my own return to wilderness.

Anne & Chekika

"Well welcome here. I'm glad you made it safely. We're almost finished with these plants, so I'll show you your room in just a minute. Please, look around and make yourself comfortable," she said, still smiling kindly as she introduced me to her other beloved and ailing German Shepherd, Chekika. Anne hustled away as quickly as she had appeared, anxious to finish the task I'd interrupted.

A quick look around her property revealed a neatly stacked mini-mountain of firewood resting against the wood shed, a small pond with a sandy bank, a lush and well tended garden, and a freshly cut lawn. An interesting array of tropical plants, much like a tiny jungle, had been plucked up and plopped down in a potting shed in the midst of the Adirondack hills rolling around us. A friend had stopped by to help Anne carry the jungle indoors. Her precious accumulation surely would not survive outdoors in the bitterly cold winter forewarned by recent cool nights. I watched them load and move one six foot tall avocado tree with what must have been at least fifty pounds of dirt holding its roots before gathering my wits enough to be of use. I had, after all, promised to help with chores during my visit. I wanted to earn my keep. We spent the better part of the next hour re-locating her jungle, plant by plant to indoor cubbyhole, window and sunbeam, until the two-story farmhouse seemed to hug its gentle arms around the exotic greenery and settle down with a contented sigh.

I felt much the same when settling into a comfortably cushioned chair on the screened porch the next day with Anne, Xandor and Chekika to conduct the interview I'll share with you now.

~~~~~~~~~~~~

Lisa: I'm here in upstate New York with Anne LaBastille, Chekika and Xandor. We're having a lovely morning on the porch looking at the beautiful mountains. Anne has been gracious enough to agree to spend some time with me here today to talk about her experiences as a woodswoman and the inspiration that she has been to so many of us.

Lisa: Anne, there are probably about four or five hundred questions that I would like to ask you today, but in the interest of your time and my book topic of women's body image and outdoor adventure, I'll keep my questions pretty focused on that. Are you feeling chipper today?

Anne: Yeah!

Lisa: I figured, you look chipper; you look beautiful. OK Xandor, lie down. Now that we got the dogs settled too, we're ready to go. Are you ready to hop right into the first question?

Anne: You bet.

Lisa: This is a question that I've actually used in my body image research with outdoorswomen. I think it's an interesting and perhaps even helpful one. That question is, in your mind, Anne, what does it take for a woman to be physically attractive?

Anne: The first and foremost is that you are clean. That doesn't mean using the roll-on antiperspirants and make up and tons of perfume. There's just the kind of clean like, well, a dip in the pond or a nice hot shower late at night. There's this feeling of having your body clean and using the minimum of make-up to accent maybe your eyelashes or something, having natural skin showing that gets all that circulation through it, and eating a good diet so you don't have blemishes and acne. I think the more natural you are as a woman the better. You can do so much with the way you wear your hair and the way your body and self look in terms of being slim and fit that you don't need to do all this other stuff that's in Cosmopolitan. One could spend $200 a month and probably not look any better.

Lisa: Kind of like Naomi Wolfe in the *Beauty Myth* cautioned us about the "magic potions" we could spends hundreds of dollars on?

Anne: Right.

Lisa: So, pond water is better?

Anne: And drinking lots of wild water. Water that's not full of chlorine and who knows what other carcinogens. Having some natural bacteria get into your system and keep your own antibodies up. Going barefoot so your feet are not full of corns or calluses. I hate that ad they have on TV.

Lisa: Oh?

Anne: They show those three women sitting on a park bench with a city behind them and they all have these corns, and they show these different corn patches and yucky feet. I think oh my Lord imagine to have to... Well, they can't help it, they live in a city and have to dress up, and they probably wear the wrong kind of shoes. But, what an awful way. It's almost as bad as a Chinese woman having her feet bound when she's two years old and hobbling around the rest of her life.

Lisa: Almost like torture?

Anne: Yes, because you're not wearing natural kind of shoes, or you're not going barefoot.

Lisa: So that's important in terms of the whole definition of physical attractiveness for you? That naturalness and the things that you do for your body and to honor yourself show beauty?

Anne: Yes, and when you feel good about yourself then maybe you project that kind of radiance or glow that other people don't have because they're miserable. Their shoes are miserable and their city clothes are miserable plus all the pancake make-up and urgency to get to the beauty parlor today at 3:00 PM and have some more dye put on their hair. When you think of it, we just kind of load our bodies up with all these artificial things, and people do it routinely week after week after week. I don't think it's chemically good for you, and it's certainly not psychologically.

Lisa: Has this clean naturalness always been your definition? Have you felt that way since childhood- since adolescence?

Anne: Yes. It's more than just being clean. I think a good tan is important. I say pooh to this SPF. You can stay in from 11:00 AM to 1:00 PM, so you don't have to put all that sun block on. I believe that human beings were made to be in the sun part of the time and that sun is good for you. It helps metabolize vitamin D in your system and helps prevent osteoporosis because it allows the calcium be metabolized. It's a chain reaction. My skin doctor has said several times, "well just keep going out in the sun and coming back to let me check you once a year. If a mole changes or something looks funny, I'll zap it off."

He says that if I look good and feel good about it, go ahead. He also says that when you're over 40-45 you need to start having more sunlight on your body because that's when your menopause might start and osteoporosis risk increases. If you're getting more sun, Vitamin D and calcium it's better for you. So I'm a big sun worshiper. Another thing that I think is real important is to stay slim, not let yourself get overweight. And that also includes being muscular. I have to go back to the fact that so many people live in cities. Almost 85% of our population is urban now, and they are locked up in these little boxes called apartments. You can't climb a tree there or hoe a garden there or chop wood there. It's all kind of butting your head against the wall. You have to really work hard at devising ways to exercise your body. And I don't think there is anything more boring than having to sit and do calisthenics. I don't even think I would like to go to a Nautilus place and pull all those machines around. Luckily I live out in a very rural and, in fact, a wild place, and I am able to use every muscle in my body in a day by just doing all kinds of different things. But I realize that 85% of the people can't do that, so you're real challenged as an urban woman. How do you get muscle tone? Where do you go to do it? Can you get away on the weekends and take a nice long hike and get fresh air in your lungs? That's a real challenge today.

Let's face it, most of our offices are all sealed up so the windows would implode if anything happened. You can't open the windows, and you're completely dependent on a huge circulation of air. You don't know where it's coming from, and you don't know how it's been filtered. You don't know what germs and pathogens are flying around. Somebody sneezes on the 10th floor; will you catch that virus down on the 3rd floor like on an airplane where you might catch any virus or cold on board? Respiration is very important to try to get fresh air in your lungs. Again, it's a real challenge to do that. I would say if you live in a city and you could open windows in your apartment or in your home at night, that's the time to get your fresh air input if you can't get in your office or gym where you might go to exercise. That could be all recirculated air, all stale. But there is nothing better than to be able to take a nice brisk walk or a hike on a crystal clear day where there's a north wind coming down out of the Arctic and Canada. All these woods up here are full of oxygen and turpentines, which you know are the aromatic oils that come from conifers. They are so good for the lungs. That's why all those TB patients were sent over the years to the Adirondacks; they could sit at the lake on a porch all wrapped in blankets and breathe these turpentines and beautiful balsa firs and crystal clean oxygen, and they'd get better partly just from that. Of course diet, medicine and other things worked, but so much of our health I think is linked to having fresh air to breathe. And I'll give you a real good example. I have a friend who does desktop publishing, and she's got her office down in the basement of her home. There are absolutely no windows there. It's all underground where they dig a hole to pour a basement and then build a house on top of it. In her office she has a computer, a laser printer, a Xerox machine, a couple of other machines; I forget what they are. We know that Xerox machines do put out ozone with the chemicals that make the copies.

Lisa: The toner? Is that what the problem is?

Anne: The heat goes over the toner and the light, and who knows? I think it's not enough to worry about usually, but my friend works in the basement for hours. Oh, the color TV, she has a color TV down there. ſhe is watching TV with one eye and typing with another eye. ſhe's very good, very skilled. ſhe has the Xerox machine on all day, and she has the computer on all day. We don't know what those gases and heating stuff are and what's in these machines and what it's doing! But, time after time after time she will have pneumonia, bronchitis and bad colds. It's gotten so now she says well, I have my fall bronchitis; I've got my winter pneumonia; I've got my spring cold. Why is she getting all that? I'm not a sinus and bronchial conditions expert, but I believe it's because she is closed up in those cement bound walls with no fresh air coming in. All she breathes all day are these fumes and stale air. I think that's affecting her lungs. This is just a small example of what I am trying to say. Fresh air is really important to keep you healthy.

Lisa: Do you recommend that people use those clean air machines? Do you think there's really any benefit?

Anne: Absolutely. In fact, I bought my friend one. I have another friend who's got one in every single room because he's bothered with allergies and pollen and stuff. He finds great relief from them. Our lives today have gotten so technological. We're dependent on that to make our living, dependent for our jobs, and we have to try to counteract the bad affects such as air pollution and noise pollution with machinery such as air filters and that background noise that you can listen to at night so that you can't hear the sirens screaming outside. I mean it's kind of a Catch-22 because you go round and round and round; you just hope you make it through your life without getting deathly sick.

Lisa: And it sounds like the life you have created so that you can live in nature and wilderness is way of caring for yourself. In addition to the care that you do for the environment and ecosystems that you have been involved in, you are caring for yourself, too.

Anne: That's true, but it's not just pampering one's body. It's also because living the kind of lifestyle I do it makes me very creative and productive. I could not write the kinds of things I do if I was in a city office. Besides having the stinky air and having all the noise out in the street, I just couldn't work there. So by creating a place that's both healthy for me and my body, I've also created a place where I'm able to be extremely productive and be very happy working. I love to get up in the morning and do what I do all day long. You know, I'm just really lucky. Because, let's face it, there's how many billion people in the world already? And if everybody went out and built a cabin in the woods there wouldn't be any woods or room.

Lisa: So your exercise has really been the hard work that you do. I mean, your life is not as cushy as the lives many other people live. Even though there are all the downsides with technology and pollution and other things that urban people are dealing with, you can choose not to have many of the conveniences. For you to keep warm is work, and for you to keep clean is work. So you get to chop wood for exercise.

Anne: It's great for upper arm strength, great for the shoulders.

Lisa: Paddling supplies to the cabin in your canoe is tremendous exercise. So is the walking that you do to get about and to haul things you need, like carrying buckets of wild water to be heated, if you even bother.

Anne: It takes two buckets of water from my lake to take a sponge and pail bath. A gallon of water is 8 pounds, so I probably have about 2 gallons in each pail to carry up the trail, or about 32 pounds.

Lisa: So you're definitely not a person who is doing push ups or clocking the miles and saying, I'm going to walk 3 miles this morning. You're not really measuring or noticing exercise in that way?

Anne: It's built into my lifestyle. And at the end of the year I go for my checkup the doctor says, Well, you look pretty fit. You look 17 years younger than you really are. I say to myself, Oh boy, I must be doing something right.

Lisa: Has your weight been pretty stable over the years?

Anne: Yes. It ranges between 112 and 120.

Lisa: Our readers are not going to see you here today. You are very slim and lightly muscular and fit looking. Sounds like your body hasn't really changed much in your lifetime.

Anne: What keeps it that way is hard work, and I mean hard work. You shovel sand, you dig holes; you chop wood, you carry heavy weights; you start outboard motors; you paddle a canoe; you take people in the wilderness with backpacks. Some people will say you're abusing yourself, and sometimes it feels like it. But you're also prolonging your life. All the old timers that I've had the privilege to know in the Adirondacks- like Rodney, the master wilderness guide I apprenticed with- were all incredibly hard workers. They never stopped. They did everything. Their hands were gnarled and their bodies were maybe injured here and injured there, but they just kept on going. They all lived into their 80's and were fit. They weren't senile, and they weren't in a nursing home. And that's the way human beings were made to be. Finally one day you just drop dead. That's better than taking the long way out- years and years of debilitating illness and being taken care of.

Lisa: So your intention is to go on as the strong healthy woodswoman you've always been until it's time to ....

Anne: I don't plan to retire. I don't plan to do anything differently. I mean, I can't tell who is going to come into my life, go out of my life, doggies and all that. The basic formula is hard work, good clean air and water, and keeping fit.

Lisa: What about your eating habits? Could you describe what you like to eat and what foods matter to you terms of your health- for helping you do what you do? I know keeping slim is important to you, as is being muscular and fit. Is there anything special about your eating habits that you would like to talk about?

Anne: Well, I eat meat- I'm a carnivore. There's a great saying in Central America where I've done some ecological research and consulting. It's from the turtle hunters down in Nicaragua. They're very strong, robust black fishermen who like to kill sea turtles, which weigh a couple hundred pounds. These hunters say that they have to have protein and that you can't make it if you're working hard on a diet that's all starchy. During the rainy season, they can't go out to sea and get turtles. They're reduced to bananas, corn and rice and a lot of starchy stuff. Not even the tropical fruits are much in season. So they have this 3 month period where they go on a soft diet. They say that they feel bad, and they feel tired. They notice that they're not getting the protein they need to do this hard work, and they start going down.

I believe in that. I always have some meat in my diet. But, I am also careful not to over do it, and I very much try to cut out fats. So I eat no-fat cottage cheese, no-fat sour cream and low-fat milk. I think dairy fat can do a lot of damage to your body and your arteries. I always try to have vegetables and some fruit during the day. And since I now have a winter place at this old farmstead, I can have my own garden. I use no pesticides and no chemical fertilizers at all. It's very good soil. I feel that's a very healthy way to have my own greens, my own corn, potatoes, carrots- all stuff I can put in the basement and store for the winter. It will keep me going. Oh, and squash; I put up a lot of squash. I also get maple syrup, and I think all that is pretty healthy. I keep Coke to a minimum even though I LOVE Classic Coke with ice in it. I never eat candy. And I start my morning with a jump-start of Cuban espresso. One a day. It's not like I'm loaded up on too much caffeine.

Lisa: So you pretty much eat good healthy whole foods; you're careful to get protein; and you avoid fats, especially dairy fats. It's sounds like other than watching your intake of dairy fats, you're eating pretty much what you want to eat, you're not restricting or.....

Anne: We don't have to be space scientists to figure this out. We can read all the statistics about Asian women. They eat so much rice and fish and have practically no breast cancer. Then they come to this country, and within one or two generations they're having breast cancer, colon cancer, and all these things. So what is going on here? I think one of the biggest... I hope I don't get shot for saying this, but I think the dairy industry has done us a disservice in hyping rich fatty products. I mean, if they want to hype skim milk or low-fat cottage cheese, fine. But it's like everybody is supposed to drink milk their whole life. If you look at any wild warm-blooded mammal, do they drink milk all the rest of their life? No. When do they drink milk? When they're a little kitten or a little puppy or whatever they are, and then they stop. They never drink it again. So, why should we?

Lisa: Good point.

Anne: You can get calcium in other ways. I mean, it just seems to me it's pretty obvious that a lot of fat comes with that dairy. I think we need to envision these arteries and veins going through our bodies like sap in a tree, bringing blood and lymph fluid around and bringing sugar to our brain and bringing energy to our muscles. If those tubes get clogged up we're in a big problem. How do they get clogged up? They get clogged up with fat and plaque. So you just keep that picture and say, how am I keeping my tubes open for the next 90 years? You get the drift of what I am trying to say?

Lisa: Exactly. How you feel and how you feed your body so that it supports your life and supports you seems more your focus than counting calories or being stuck to a certain kind of diet. You're feeding yourself in order to support your life. What do you think about diets- even just here in the United States- because it's common for many women, especially these days, to try all the different diet programs available?

Anne: I think it's a whole bunch of horse feathers. All you have to do is put your fork down.

Lisa: That simple?

Anne: That's where it all starts. If that fork goes in your mouth too often, you're going to get fat, and you're going to have a hard time taking it off. I don't know many of my friends who have been overweight and went on diets who ever took it off and stayed slim. It seems like a see-saw, see-saw. I just say leave the fork on the table and get up and walk away. It takes a terrific self-control, but look at the bad things that will happen if you don't do it. You risk the loss of self-image.

Lisa: So what role do you think that physical effectiveness has played, if any, in your sense of being physically attractive?

Anne: Well, I don't think physical attractiveness is the point. I think it's being professionally effective. When you're physically fit I think you get a certain way of walking, and a certain way of carrying yourself and a certain place your head is at. You start walking tall, and you look like you know who you are, and you look assertive. Nobody is going to mess around with you. I think that's very important for several reasons. First of all, women have been victims so often that you need to show even with the way you walk and take care of yourself that you're not going to put up with that.

Another reason: let's say you go to a conference and share papers. You would go up on the stage and have a microphone and be stoop shouldered, looking around timidly. Even if you're excited, you are not going to present your message well. Your lecture, or class or whatever is going to be 100% more effective if you're standing straight up, speaking out and looking like you're enjoying it. Or at least you're going to get through it, and it's not going to be a bad job. I just see so many women like this. I go around lecturing mostly and doing workshops, and I see that they're apologizing for themselves all the time. They're kind of a little bit hunched over, and they're not looking you in the eye. Two very important things about a physically fit person are that you have a straight steady gaze, and you're not afraid to look at somebody. A lot of people can't handle eye contact. It's so important even just to make a first friend, or make a first impression in a job or with a higher up in your career. The other thing is shaking hands. You make a very good impression if you put your hand right smack in the other person's and don't do a little fish tail, and you sure don't want to crush the cartilage of some poor 80-year-old person whose arthritis screams. You do a nice, palm-to-palm clasp that's firm but not painful. It says I'm not afraid of you; I'm a strong person, and I'm happy to meet you. And look 'em in the eye. I think that does a whole lot of breaking the ice and making an impression that is favorable. At least this should work in America. It may not work in Japan or Iran or some other country where people may not understand what it means when you are that forward.

Lisa: Especially with women, at least in my experience. So what I'm wondering then, is demeanor part of what you mean by professional effectiveness? Your demeanor—does it speak well of you? does it speak of your strength and confidence? Maybe for you it's a given that you will be able to do your chores at least for the most part throughout your life. But your demeanor can help demonstrate to others the professional effectiveness you are talking about?

Anne: That's right. It's important for women to have professional skills, because so many men still think they can't do anything outdoors. You can't run an outboard motor; you can't start a snow mobile or you can't run a chainsaw; you can't build a cabin. Let's use the example of doing research in another country. If I go there to talk with somebody in their Department of Environmental Conservation and try to convince them to make a wildlife refuge, let's say, and I can talk and talk and have all kinds of statistics and reasons why. But if that person knows that I run a boat and I completed a census that took five days and worked through big waves and wind by night and by day. If they understand that I am a wildlife person, and I know what to do with binoculars, and I know how to run all the machinery that goes along with my profession, then I'm much more effective. Having those skills is a kind of proof that you know what you're talking about; it's not just research.

Lisa: I'm thinking about what it must have been like for you so many times to go to meet government officials, or non-government officials, and to have to present yourself as this person coming from so far away and having all these things to talk about- like at Lake Atilan. You need permissions and have all these complex things to do. If your demeanor had been timid or your way of presenting yourself had been anything other than appropriately assertive and appropriately courteous and appropriately confident, I think that would have been problematic. I can see where that would be a tremendous asset for you in your professional presentation of effectiveness.

Anne: I'm glad you used the word *appropriately*, because sometimes women go too far. They start acting like Paul Bunyan or like some big powerful person. Then they really can over do the handshake, or they really can come across too forceful. It's HI, IT'S GOOD TO MEET YOU, HI, JOE HOW ARE YOU? That's not appropriate to being a woman either. I believe it's important to keep your femininity and to keep a gentleness and ladylike demeanor. What's wrong with wearing nail polish on your feet or putting a squirt of perfume on your ear?

Lisa: Exactly, lipstick on when your lips are chapped - or even if they're not chapped, like yours right now.

Anne: Those things also make you believable. You're still a nice woman; you have a good handshake, and you have these skills and calluses on your hands. It makes a nice package, I think.

Lisa: I think maybe what we're talking about is individual balance. You have your balance of strength and your balance of femininity. Strength can be part of femininity, of course. You can look like a woman, it's just that you're a strong woman.

Anne: That's it!

Lisa: I think a lot of people that you've inspired for so long would be really interested in any advice or guidance you could give us about getting out in nature and doing things and empowering us to believe in ourselves. You probably have quite a few readers and fans that are older now, you know, approaching their 40's, 50's and maybe even more. Are there some words that you could share with us about that as we change and our bodies change?

Anne: It's a new route every single year. It's kind of new in my thinking, this getting older. It's a challenge. I hear daily, *daily* -from employees, employers and friends- there is always this thing in America about aging, aging, aging. Like one of the recent surgeries I had on my shoulder: I can't tell you how many people said, Well, of course, if you were younger it would heal up sooner. I say for God's sake don't talk about that. Age is not what's making it not heal up; it got damaged badly in an accident. It's always the big excuse: you're getting older; you're falling apart. I hate it. You don't hear that in Latin America. The older you get the more you're revered and appreciated, the wiser you are, and the more you are helped here and there. It's a beautiful experience to get older down there, but up here it's like: You're 45? Throw 'em on the fish pile.

I fight that every step of the way. If somebody starts in I just give it back to 'em' and say: I'm getting better; I wouldn't go back one day. Would you go back to being 16 again? NO WAY, nothing back there. I like where I am, and I like what I'm doing. I have a symbol that came to me on this farm. I have this small falcon that comes here to nest. It's a kestrel. It's the smallest one of our falcons. People think of hawks and falcons as being these huge eagles, raptors and vultures, but this is the most adorable, pretty, slim, defiant little critter. It flies up in the air and glitters; they are just beautiful. It has a kind of a salmon color breast with light gray in the back. It's one of my favorite birds. I watched them here on the farm as they made their nest and swooped around in their aerial courtship. I just fell in love with these kestrels. The female is the dominant bird because she is bigger than the male, and she's quite aggressive. I said, I'd like to be like that kestrel. They're small like I am, and they're slim like I am, but they're defiant...

Lisa: Like you are!

Anne: Yes, I've learned to be like that. Kestrels symbolize this. They are free to fly up in the air, do all these wonderful displays, and they are wonderful parents. They're my symbol for the aging process: Be like the kestrel. Stay small; stay slim; stay strong. They are so strong they can swoop down and pick up a mouse or pick up a rat or pick up a grasshopper and tear it apart and give it to their chickies. I have a chapter in my new book *Woodswoman III* called 'Like a Kestrel.' I get on a soap box and say all the stuff I've been saying to you. Don't let people put you down because you're getting older. In fact, women over 45, particularly after they are done with menopause, are the most productive people in our society. They're not going to have kids; they don't have to worry about all that courtship business and finding a mate; and maybe their husbands died and left them a million dollars. They can do all the things that they want to do. If they want to go back to school and get a Ph.D., if they want to adopt a poor orphan, if they want to get into a new profession they probably have the time, the money and the motivation to do that.

My big plea in that chapter, "Like A Kestrel" is for women who want to help the world to become fierce ecofeminists. I don't care how you do it. Go out and take kids on a nature walks; go study elephants in Africa like Cynthia Moss did; go help volunteer at a national park. But it shouldn't be that you're only going to volunteer. You're not going to be a "pink lady" for the rest of your life. You're going to get paid for this. You're going to get expert in this. You're going to be in demand....consulting and advising. You are going to be on boards. There are something like 400 conservation groups in this country. You could get on a board of a nature conservation group and really have a say-so in the policies on how these foundations and agencies reach out to save wildlife and wildlands. So that's my hope. Older women will get into the environmental field and make a mark to save our planet.

Lisa: So we should be like kestrels. Isn't that wonderful! Do you think you're beautiful, Anne?

Anne: No.

Lisa: You don't? Have you ever felt that way- that you're beautiful?

Anne: No.

Lisa: How would you describe yourself then? I think most people would completely disagree with you on that, but...why do you say that you're not beautiful?

Anne: Well because I have my vision of what's a beautiful woman, and I don't fit that at all. I think maybe I'm cute when I have a suntan and freckles and my muddy bare feet and my baseball cap and my old blue jeans on. You know, I fit a kind of tomboyish, cute image. That's all I want. I'm not trying to be like- I don't know who...gorgeous-- well, like Linda Evans. She's really beautiful.

Lisa: So you really don't think you are beautiful. Well that surprises me. I'm sitting here wondering if you say that because you don't want to sound arrogant?

Anne: It's not important to me to be beautiful, and I don't think I am. It's more important that I'm productive and a good writer. That's the way it is. But I have my own kind of endearing ways...

Lisa: Absolutely. And you have your confident demeanor, and the other part of that effectiveness that it takes for someone to be physically attractive. You are all those things personified: the fit, the lean, the muscular. So I guess maybe that doesn't necessarily mean stereotypically "beautiful" for you.

Anne: Beauty can be a real hazard. If you're beautiful, you may be perceived as less intelligent.

Lisa: Taken less seriously, perhaps?

Anne: Unless you're a millionaire. Then you might combine beauty and money and do really useful things. I would like to be beautiful and a millionaire because I could go out and buy national parks and set up game reserves and hire people to take care of endangered species. It would be terrific; boy I'd have a good time. Dream on, Anne.

Lisa: I have two more questions for you, Anne, just briefly. I think to a great degree you have already answered this first question, just to make sure though, I'll ask it now. What do you think has been the influence of your experiences as an outdoorswoman on your feelings about your body?

Anne: I think I'm really fortunate because I have two things going for me at once. One of them is the fact that my lifestyle is a very physical and active way of keeping in fairly good shape. But I also have this other thing going for me, and it's the image that I have created with my books on being a woodswoman. A lot of it is fantasy in people's minds, but it still is nevertheless true. I didn't fake it that I built a cabin, nor live at the edge of wilderness.

Lisa: It feels very real to me with you today, I can tell you that.

Anne: What it gives to me, I think, is a certain edge that I've reached that I don't see in a lot of other people. I see it in maybe one other woman friend who is also a licensed guide for the Adirondacks. And I see it sometimes in young women today just getting out of college that have been exposed and given every opportunity and are in male fields and pushing their way through. You come to a point where your body reacts in certain automatic ways, and more importantly, your mind pushes you to do something. I could go around with you and you would think I was so polite and such a nice lady and slim and fit and all that. But suddenly there would be this emergency- and I've seen this over and over and over again with women in workshops- something will happen that we have to immediately respond to. Most of them just sort of shrink back, and they don't know what to do. But I just jump right into it, and the thought of getting hurt or anything never enters my mind. There is kind of animal like instinct that takes over, and it's a combination of courage and knowing you're strong enough to get into this. Maybe a combination of sheer fearlessness and a whole bunch of things wrapped into one; it has come through these years and years of conditioning your body. You can't really walk tall until you know that you've got that.

I'm trying to think of an example... Maybe you pass a wreck on the road, and you stop and rush out to help that person. Maybe you've been trained as an EMT, but the fact is that you stopped and you leapt in and you tried to be useful. Another example could be in the woods: somebody suddenly got hurt and was lying there. You have to go out and immediately figure how to make a stretcher, decide who is going to carry it and figure how far is it out. You're the one to run as fast as you can to get to a car and tell em' to come help....

Lisa: And then remain calm and steady as you do it and know that you're doing what needs to be done.

Anne: But it's sometimes also violent physical acts. I remember once I was down in the Amazon basin doing an article assignment for *Audubon* magazine. I tell about this in my latest book, *Jaguar Totem*. We had been taken in by helicopter to this magnificent huge national park. It was mostly oil companies traveling in and out of there, because they were the only people who were anywhere near this part of the country. We were at one point, to give you an idea of the remoteness, 100 miles by dugout canoe from the nearest settlement. There were eight of us that had gone down from Washington, D.C., all conservationists. We're waiting; they're having to ferry us out 2 by 2 by 2, so I was with one of the men and one of the first ones out. We're waiting near a gigantic Hercules Transport four engine plane that had brought in bulldozers and stuff for the oil drilling. All of a sudden another helicopter came rushing in, and we thought it was the rest of our crew, but they were bringing in a man who had been injured. He had been out cutting the lines that they have to have for the trail. He had fallen backward and impaled himself on a sharp stick; it had just cut up his anus.

Lisa: Oh-h-h-h gosh...

Anne: He was all bleeding inside. I imagined a fearful bacterial infection. They took him out of the helicopter and put him on a stretcher and rushed him into the Hercules. Well, there was nobody in the Hercules. All the bulldozers had come out. It was just this big huge empty cargo plane with no windows and oil and dirt and filth all over the floor because they hauled heavy equipment all the time. The pilots were trying to rush back to Lima to get back into Peru. They had to get back before dark, and they had to go from the jungle side of the Andes to the Pacific coast. And here's this poor Indian just lying there ashen faced. They asked one of the engineers if he could go with him, but the guy said he couldn't go because he had to stay with his men who were drilling. I suddenly just jumped up and said *I'll go with him; I'm an EMT!* Thank goodness I had taken that course.

Eventually we all had to go back there anyway. There was just no question in my mind as I jumped in the plane. I spoke a little Spanish and said to the guy, *Don't worry, it's going to be all right*. I could at least take his vital signs and know where he's at when we get to the airport. Here I was all by myself in this, scared to fly to begin with. I couldn't see out the window, and this guy is on the stretcher.

Lisa: You were on the Hercules Transport?

Anne: Yes, then they shut up the doors in the back. It's like these little teeny lights come on, and the first thing I notice this guy is lying on the floor with nothing to hold him to the stretcher. I had to go scrounging around all this oil and filth to find some wire to lash him down; there were rings and stuff all around for the machinery. Then I just sat by him and just kept taking his pulse and saying he was going to be all right. I kept stroking his head and trying to calm him and making sure he wasn't going into shock or anything. He was very quiet. He was probably scared shitless!

Lisa: I can imagine-not to mention the pain.

Anne: It was getting darker outside, so I finally left him for a minute after telling him I would be right back. I wanted to go up and see where the pilots were in this big flying box. I went up to where I knew they had to be- in the front of the plane and up somewhere high. There was a little ladder, so I climbed up and came through this teeny door. There were two pilots. I looked out the window; we had left the jungle. There was an incredible white mass of mountain and glaciers and rock, and the sun was just setting into the west toward the Pacific. That orange light was flooding down, and all below us was purple dark. It was the most magnificent view I've probably ever seen.

The pilots greeted me and invited me up front where they asked how my patient was doing. Just as I was updating them, I saw the highest mountain in the western hemisphere. You know it was just...whew! I told the pilot I had to go back and watch our patient after he told me we'd be at the airport in 20 minutes. I went back and sat with him until they landed this huge big thing and a bunch of guys ran in and took him off the floor. They took him out, but there was no ambulance- nothing. So I went with him. The airport was closed down, and it was dark now. They laid him down on this cement, and I sat down next to him. They said, *Oh someone will be along.*

Everybody went home because they had shut off the engines and the pilots had left. I'm sitting with this poor guy in this windy cold airport, and eventually an ambulance came and took him away. I never heard what happened to him. I never had any feedback; I didn't have the names of the pilots; I never thought to get a number to call to find out about him. It was just one of those freak things that happened. I volunteered- jumped into it and did my good deed for that poor guy. He could have died the next day from massive infections. Who knows what happened, or if they operated on him in time.

Lisa: But you had whatever it took to jump right in and that's what...

Anne: That's the quality I'm talking about.

Lisa: My final question for now: will you talk to us a little bit about what having that preparedness and being in the wilderness means to you?

Anne: That's an important point, Lisa. Wilderness gives me that kind of edge. When you are out in true wilderness- I'm talking about a place that is very large, has no roads, no buildings, no engines like the 1.1 million acres of legally classified wilderness in the 6 million acre Adirondack Park- you can't mess up. You have to accept that you're not very important out there. There are no signs of human touches, and you've got to tread softly, carefully and enjoy it. It is a wonderful feeling to be out there with nobody else around and no noise. I mean how often in your life do you go a day without hearing a gas engine?

Lisa: Hardly ever.

Anne: Well, that's not good for people. There's something about silence. It's very, very healing. By going out in the wilderness, which is my favorite thing to do, camping or canoeing I re-establish, I re-energize that certain place in myself that makes me self reliant. If something goes wrong, I can't run down to the hardware store. For food, I've got to see if there is something around to eat, and if there's not I have to change my plans or go hungry. You can die in a short while particularly in the winter, but I never go wilderness camping in the winter. It's dangerous. So that's one reason why I live in a cabin that backs up to a 50,000 acre wilderness track. Maybe I wouldn't go there for a year. Let's say I was too busy writing books or going around lecturing. But the fact is that it is there. In the final analysis, if I just want to get away from it all-go back to recharge, I can go. It's like my church, a counselor's couch, everything wrapped into one except you don't need those things. You don't need those artificial humanized institutions and psychotherapy and religion and all the other stuff we do to try to get through this hard life. I just go back there, and if it's good weather and I can stay a few days, it is very calming. I get great ideas about things to write, and I can make up poems inside my head. I go barefoot all the time, and I stay in the sun all the time. I'm just as natural as I can be. I go skinny dipping and all the things that human beings were made to do, and that's very healthy.

Lisa: Thank you so very much Anne. This has just been a delight. Is there anything I didn't ask that I should have?

Anne: We've got to preserve those wildernesses for people like me who need to go there. It's no different than saying: *Oh did you hear that they are going to tear down the Metropolitan Museum of Art in New York City? There are big plans to demolish and put a baseball field in there.* You'd be frantic and say *Oh, my gosh, art is the most important thing in the world. We have to save it!*

If you tell me you're going to go and sell off my wilderness and put condos out there, or amusement parks and waterslides, I would say,

Hey wait a minute, a lot of people need that just the way you like to go see the Mona Lisa or Van Gogh. I need to go out there and see that 300 -year-old pine tree and rock with moss all over it, yellow, green and orange. I love to ski over the ice on Black Bear Lake and watch the moon come up on a cold night. That is just as beautiful to me as paintings. And, I have just as much right to have my wilderness museum as people have to go an art museum.

Lisa: So your preservation work and passion shall continue?

Anne: I hope so.

Thank you very much Anne for the interview, for my unforgettable visit, for our growing friendship and for the inspiration you continue to provide so many of us. May your days in wild places be many, healthy and peaceful.

**Lisa, Anne & Xandor
after the interview**

Questions for Reflection

1. How does Anne's definition of physical attractiveness compare to media ideals for physical attractiveness?

2. What impact do you think that Anne's rejection of some societal norms for women has had on her body image?

3. What would you call that "quality" that Anne is trying to name?

4. Is this quality one that you have, too? And if so, how does it relate to your sense of feeling "beautiful" or "physically attractive?"

WHAT IS BEAUTY: AN EXPLORATION OF SELF AND CONNECTION

Allison Bradley

What is beauty?

How would I know if I was beautiful? What data would lead to this conclusion? Would it come from me?

Would it come from people around me? Would it come from the interaction between us?

These are the questions that coursed through me as I tromped through the woods one hot July afternoon, leading a group of seventh grade students on to their next outdoor challenge. The group of six boys and five girls had just finished a Spider Web. A young woman in the group stood out during the activity. She actively helped lift everyone else through the web. She cheered and clapped and gave supportive commentary. She deflected questions about when she would like to go, waiting until last. She looked away and did not accept physical support when it was her turn. She called herself "heavy." She said that supporting her would be "too hard" for the others. When others in the group thanked her for her help, she minimized her contribution, saying that the others were "good at it anyway," and that she "didn't really do anything."

The activity reached a natural conclusion, and the group processed their experiences. As I listened to this young woman talk, I heard questions about who she was and why she mattered. I heard a need for connection strangely and desperately linked with a need to define her own person. I heard the fear, rage, and sorrow of one trapped by external circumstances and expectations yet unable to find the means or strength to create new ones. I heard confusion about where she ends and where others begin...to whom she is responsible, and what that might mean. I heard the need to escape having her body be a focal point of discussion and discernment, the need to not have to worry about whether or not she "looks good enough" or whether she is "heavy," "thin," or anything in-between. I heard the voice of many women, young and old, of all shapes, sizes and colors. It is a familiar voice. Its echoes ring in all of us.

Were someone to say to this young woman, "Please describe yourself in one word," I wonder what it would take for her to feel inspired to answer, "Beautiful."? I wonder what it would take for that larger voice, the one representing all women, to answer in the affirmative as well. What would it take for our programs to help this young woman and others like her?

I begin, as with any legitimate questioning process, by asking myself. "Please describe yourself in one word." "Well…." attempts the hesitant internal response, "…it depends." Labels and categories struggle to align themselves in my mind: Mother, Friend, Athlete, Wife, Ph.D., Homeowner, Life- Threatening Disease Survivor, Domestic Violence Activist, Adventure Facilitator, Lover, Dissident…the list tumbles on endlessly, haphazardly, resulting at last in the question, "Who wants to know, anyway?" It is an elemental question of how I define my roles in different contexts.

The answer, of course, is me. I want to know. But even in the solitude of this questioning, I cannot escape my inherent relatedness to others.

"Am I beautiful?" continues the persistent internal voice, driving hard for a conclusion from somewhere within the onslaught of information about the various roles that I play in my life, the purposes I serve for other people and institutions. Yes, I conclude. I am beautiful. But how do I know this? The answer to this question is dauntingly complex. How do I define, understand, contextualize beauty? It seems that every reference point I have for myself is linked to someone or something else. I am reminded of Carol Gilligan's work in the area of women's development, which points to the psychological crises in women's lives as stemming from a sense of disconnection (Gilligan, 1982). How then, continues my questioning process, have I concluded that I am beautiful, given these constant connections? Do I assess myself for beauty under different circumstances at different times, like checking my pulse or my breathing, using the situationally appropriate standards of measure each time? For example, if I look in the mirror at 4:00 AM and see a mother with dark circles under her eyes and gnarled hair gently singing a lullaby to her baby, do I see beauty? If I notice a new line on my face and think about the last fifteen times I've cried, do I see beauty? If I look at my high school graduation photograph, do I see beauty? If I imagine myself leading a group of corporate executives through an experiential activity, do I see beauty? And what if the group was composed of single mothers?

Further, what do I do with this matter of connection to others in varying contexts being so elemental to who I am? I can, for example, wholly immerse myself in a personally genuine way in a given experience, but how does that affect my deep connections to others? I can fully devote my mind, body, and emotions to a fourteen-day wilderness program with at-risk youth and experience dramatic results, but what about my own children who have been at home in the meantime? Conversely, I can invest myself thoroughly in parenting, setting firm emotional and time limits on my time spent at work. How, then, do I respond to my adventurous colleagues who say I'm not emotionally or circumstantially available enough to "support the culture?" Stephanie Dowrick (1991) points to this elemental dilemma for women in *Intimacy and Solitude*:

She is aware of what other people need and turning her back on that may be more than she is capable of doing. And even when the woman rebels, she can quickly be accused of 'spoiling things for everyone' (p. 110).

The potential for paralysis in these questions is huge. It causes me to wonder how I made it through the various phases of my life without collapsing from exhaustion, or worse yet, forsaking some part of myself. The answers to these questions seem to be like biological cells, constantly giving and receiving life-creating information from the environment. They morph and flux in constant adaptation, while always maintaining some version of their essential structure.

But, how do I as an individual woman know what my own "cells" are? In other words, how do I find answers based on an autonomous sense of self that is at the same time closely related to others? The starting points for responding to this question are no doubt as varied and uniquely distinctive as the clients we serve in our programs. It is precisely because we encounter these matters with our clients, and within ourselves, that we need to consider our responses and further our understanding.

Priest and Gass describe experiential education as learning by doing with reflection, going on to describe the belief that people learn best by direct and purposeful contact with their learning experiences (Priest & Gass, 1997). If we are responsible experiential educators, it is our job to facilitate this "direct and purposeful contact" to the best of our ability. Perhaps it is valuable to look at this notion through the lens I've described in this article. How can we best facilitate programming which supports women's direct and purposeful contact with their questions about definition of "self" in relation to "connection?" How can our programming help women integrate body image successfully with a healthy sense of self?

As I think about this in my own experience as a woman, one thing becomes clear. A key element in my development has been experiencing my sense of self. Examples of experiencing my sense of self might be reflecting on journal writing, creating a sculpture or story, meditating, or clearly and honestly representing myself in conversation with others. While this may seem like a simple idea, the real life barriers to it can be tremendous. For example, setting aside an hour a day to meditate may seem impossible when one has a career, family, and other life responsibilities. However, without "protected" time and space to experience my sense of self, I have no internal reference point. I have no way to know who "I" really am, who I want to be, how I want to look, what I want to do, and so on. In the absence of a clearly understood sense of self, I may allow myself to be defined by the external influences in my life. In creating and protecting this reflective space for myself, it can seem as if I am always saying /No to something or someone important to me. In fact, my reflective space often requires the ferocious mother bear-ish protection of several /Nos to several people or circumstances. The cost of avoiding this /No, however, is more than I can afford. Knowing who I am and representing that person in the world is central to my sense of beauty as a person. It is much more important than how I look.

These matters of self, connection, and self-concept have often seemed isolating in the struggles they present. I am fortunate to have a group of strong female friends and a sensitive, insightful husband with whom I can explore these topics. Many women do not have these benefits. I, at times in my life, have not had these benefits. The exploration and struggle of self and connection have continued nonetheless. This causes me to wonder what we can do to de-isolate this experience for women, so that a larger community of support can be experienced. I wonder what we can do to "normalize" the experience of exploration of self/connection/self-concept issues such that it is woven into daily life and routine programming. I wonder what we can do to create opportunities for women. Carrying this idea further, it is possible to look at implications for experiential and adventure program facilitation. What can we do to help the women in our programs, such as the young woman described at the beginning of this article, explore who they are within their own "cells"?

Listed below are some important questions for facilitators to consider in their outdoor adventure and experiential education programming for women:

* Are active listening skills consistently used when women explore "self" and "connection" issues?

* Is a point made of checking with women and girls about personal feelings when they take responsibility for group or interpersonal dynamics?

* Is personal reflection time (for journaling, walking, meditating, etc.) built into the program?

* Is communication about "self" and "connection" issues structured in, or explicitly suggested in our programs?

* Do we use language that goes beyond "boundary setting," creating an environment in which women are safe exploring the many ways in which they might experience "self" and "connection?"

* Do debriefing and processing questions support exploration of defining "self" in relation to "other?" Are they open-ended enough to leave room for different ways of responding?

* Are the many ways women's "cells" can be compromised, from domestic violence to professional sexual harassment, readily acknowledged as real issues for women?

* Does every facet of the program, both subtle and explicit, from phone answering to programmatic leadership, both subtle and explicit, represent equity and accountability for both genders?

These and other challenging questions are just one way of holding ourselves accountable to supporting the women in our programs, as well as supporting ourselves. As each woman builds her source of internal reference, so she builds her capacity to connect effectively with others. It is my hope that experiential programs and facilitators of all kinds will continue to strengthen awareness and sensitivity to the struggle of self-concept faced by so many women.

Perhaps eventually our contributions will increase the likelihood that more women will answer that "one word" question easily, simply, and decisively: *beautiful*.

References

Dowrick, S. (1991). *Intimacy and solitude: Balancing closeness and independence.* New York, NY: W.W. Norton & Company, Inc.

Gilligan, C. (1982). *In a different voice: Psychological theory and women's development.* Cambridge, MA: Harvard University Press.

Priest, S. & Gass, M. (1997). *Effective leadership in adventure programming.* Champagne, IL: Human Kinetics.

Questions for Reflection

1. How does the author's exploration of beauty, self and connection relate to your experience in the development of your sense of yourself as a physical being?

2. What specific changes and/or additions do you think would be important to implement in outdoor adventure programming to address these issues for trip participants?

3. What would an ideal outdoor adventure education program for both male and female guides and program facilitators need to include to adequately address body image and eating disorder issues that trip participants may bring with them?

Chapter II. Exploring

LOYALSOCK TRAIL

Sylvia J. Cole

We headed out from Lycogis Girl Scout camp with no idea what our pre-teen bodies could do if we pushed them. Like turtles with our bulging pack-shells, we took our first steps into the wild.

I'm sure I charged ahead and tried to talk to the counselor in the lead; she was probably 20 but seemed so much older. We trudged, sang and checked out the animal tracks. We warmed our faces and tanned on the rocks by the stream where we'd stopped for lunch. We told our stories, traded families, made stuff up. My hands were stained with wild blueberries, learning what could be eaten to survive in the woods like a black bear.

As the light faded, our pack-shells grew heavier, binding to our hips and backs in the late afternoon. Wisely, our women counselor guides sought their destinations, teaching us to pitch camp/tents before dusk or whining set in. How many times since have I marked the ritual of wood gathering and fire building? It was here at age 10 that the first sense of girl, woman, initiate tending the hearth took hold.

We stirred, cooked and sang. Funny how your taste buds adjust to the strange proteins that float into every dish when you are trail-weary and truly hungry from a day's hiking. We learned to be a family. We learned the girl scout codes "Make new friends, but keep the old. . . one is silver and the other gold." We heard pack it out and leave no trace. Strung up our left over food in a tree to try to avoid late night pilfering by raccoon or bear.

At night, by the campfire those young women who led us, women with funny nicknames like Tweet, Mert, Jungle Jane or Amazon Annie. . . . they looked strong and bold, no lines of age yet in their faces but still prone to jumping at an owl's hoot. I felt so safe.

My light feet in moccasins tapped to the cricket metronome. The fireflies danced on the cinders swirling up to the stars. How those women knew just when to let us play in the stream or wrap up a turned ankle and said just the right soothing thing to the girl who looked homesick for days. When we came to the swaying Rope Bridge over the creek, they cracked jokes to get that last terrified kid across.

At night those women tried to hide their affection for one another, but I was observant even then. . . how someone knew what their special friend liked in her coffee in the morning. The memories stick with me now like toasted marshmallows that I smushed into ∫'mores. I share them over city-life brunches. I was that tomboy girl, bandanna on her head, who wanted to rebel over the restrictions of shoes or shirt. I was the one up in the trees.

We would stay up late trying to scare each other and conform our spines to every root and rock. ∫ome of us were farm girls who branched out with our first flex of freedom from Mennonite country ways. The few city girls were scared of the dark but already had mysterious to me, visits from some monthly "friend" and chests.

I was easily impressed with the counselors who could wield an ax or scale up a rock face. In my pre-teen curiosity I began to weave tales in my mind about these daring women. My swimmer, athletic body was challenged with new ways to stretch. I was a sprinter but sensed these were lessons for the long haul.

When the moon rose at night over the horizon and the faces became shadows, I had my dreams of staying young forever. But those women proved to me that there were reasons to want to be a grown-up. They planted the seeds in our little Girl ∫cout garden-minds. To grow up solid, assertive, out on our own in the woods with the elements and our wits.

I would tell the tales of those trips backpacking the trails of Pennsylvania- Penn's woods to my Grandmother, and only now do I truly understand the wistful-weary way she smiled. My mother has told me since that she could never have imagined being out there alone, all women on a week long hike or canoe trip.

We sang and laughed into the treetops. They swayed and answered back, "This is for the lost ones," the women who tilled the soul and sweated their freedom away so that we could fly. There I am in the picture from that Lycogis summer, snap frozen at tomboy age 10, hanging in the branches of a huge tree back at main camp wearing an "Ecology Now" shirt with a peace sign flag on the front. Our strong rooted counselor/guides are at the base.

Questions for Reflection

1. How did this early outdoor experience impact the author?

2. What do you think of these counselor/guides as role models for girls and young women?

3. What outdoor experiences and/or role models have been important in your development?

GRAND CANYON JOURNEY IN TWO VOICES

T.A. Loeffler

Kaibab the layer that most people see
(A beautiful canyon, a divided woman)
Toroweap I get the first glimpse of me,
(You're big, you're ugly, you're fat)
Coconino cliffs reach out to greet,
(You can't do this, why are you here?)
Hermit the first red rock I meet,
(Pulse is bounding, breathing deep)
Supai slopes mark the journey in,
(Quads absorb the pounding feet)
Redwall where the nightmares begin,
(Fear surrounds, the abyss calls)
Mauve signals the beginning of the end,
(Fight him off, the image falls)
Bright Angel my pack becomes a friend,
(With each step, new muscle builds)
Tapeats marks the top of the plateau
(This canyon makes the inner divide fill)
Vishnu means there is not fu rther
down to go.
(A divided canyon, a beautiful woman).

As I journey up once again, I hope this internal bridge will forever stand.

1. What "bridge" did this author construct?

2. If you were to build one of your own, what would you need?

3. How do you think this nature experience impacted the author?

4. If you could construct an ideal society or a healthy context for girls and women to collectively have a more positive body image, what would need to be present?

SHIFTING DESIRES

Molly Benson Prince

I have always been conscious of my body. For some reason, or more probably, for many reasons, at an early age I internalized the assumption that I should find success in athletics, and succeeding in athletics meant having a very thin body. Throughout high school and college, I ran track and cross-country; needless to say, neither of these sports challenged the message that successful people are thin. Though lean and sinewy, I lived in fear of growing fat. Often I ran not for the joy or freedom I could find in the activity, but because I thought I had to burn off that extra bagel, scoop of ice cream, or piece of pizza. Like many college-age women today, I became obsessed with my weight, size, and body image. Although I'm saddened now to think of the fun, happiness, and personal growth I gave up in those years simply because I felt I had to devote my energy to maintaining a super-thin body, I've seen that the curious force of life often gives us a second chance to get things right. With a few years of learning, I've come to see my body as my tool. Like any tool, this wonderful contraption is not to be kept attractive for acceptance by others, but to be cared for kindly so that it can serve me well, taking me deep into woods, high up on mountains, and quietly through deserts.

With twenty-twenty hindsight, I know that the mistaken belief in "salvation through thinness" etched itself into my mind, actions, and dreams because my early experiences never opposed the desirability of thinness. Social scientists continue to document the extensive cultural influences assailing young people, young women in particular, with the message that thinness is a must. My ears and mind tuned into those messages like a deer to the hunter, sensing danger but paralyzed to act. I cannot remember a coach, teacher, friend, sibling, or parent ever saying, "It's okay not to be super thin. It's also desirable to be strong, sturdy, and solid." I never considered the validity of such a thought until I left college, started teaching, and spent my first summer "off" on an outdoor course for educators.

This three-week course, led by two women and one man, changed drastically my thoughts about my own and others' bodies. The first changes in my thoughts, however, were only exchanges of values about the desirable body. I began not to want toned muscles, but BIG muscles. Those big muscles would mean strength, and that strength would mean the ability to lift a bigger pack, climb a tougher route, and get down a dicier boulder field. Not only did I begin to see the desirability of muscle bulk, I also began to see the value of fat. If I did not want to be cold on a three-degree night, I had better add cheese to my macaroni and margarine to my hot chocolate. In fact, if I wanted to really stay warm, I ought to add a little permanent insulation to my body. What a revelation to me!

Although personal experience was a great teacher for those new thoughts about my body, so too were the two female instructors on the course. For the first time, I was hearing "successful" women say that they wanted to "bulk up," that they were afraid of losing too much weight, and that they hoped they could keep their strong quadriceps throughout the slow winter season. Their example helped those two thoughts, " bulk is good" and "fat can be helpful," stick with me long after the course ended.

What also stuck with me was my new romance: I had fallen deeply in love with the outdoors and wanted to be more involved. In the seven years since that first course, I have celebrated more and more as an outdoor enthusiast, leader, and follower. As I reflect on the effects of this time spent outdoors, I see significant changes in my evaluation of my physical self. The first shift, alluded to earlier, is that I no longer see my body as something I should "keep attractive" for acceptance by others; instead I see my body as a tool that I should care for kindly so that I can use it for my own enjoyment, hiking further, climbing higher, venturing deeper. That shift, from "my body for others" to "my body for myself," reflects a stronger personal confidence, competence, and self-reliance.

Time spent outdoors has also pulled me quickly to self-acceptance. Before becoming involved in outdoor pursuits, my athletic endeavors had always meant competing against others – Who had the fastest time, highest jump, quickest start? That competitive environment also fueled a competitive body awareness – Who had the thinnest waist, longest legs, leanest body? The outdoor arena, however, emphasizes cooperation, not competition. As the desire to compete and win began to fade, in its place has grown a desire to find harmony with others, with nature, and eventually, with myself. I do not profess to have lost all desire to compete, but time in the outdoors has shown me the value of harmony and the limited rewards of competition.

Active involvement in outdoor pursuits has also opened my eyes to the diversity and imperfection in nature. Our modern vocabulary often gives words such as "imperfection" and "diversity" pejorative meanings, while extolling the value of uniformity. Grocers advertise their produce as free of imperfection; schools worry over diverse student bodies while corporate firms strive to duplicate the success of their competitors; and city planners strive for uniformity in their communities. But in nature, diversity and imperfection create a self-sustaining and dynamic balance. While backpacking in the Oregon and Washington Cascades, I saw old growth forest that, due to age and specie diversity, survived an often fatal beetle infestation. A few trees perished, but the vast majority of flora and fauna survived. Near that same area, I also saw Christmas tree farms destroyed entirely by a single-tree virus. Because the trees on those farms lacked diversity in their ages and species, they were all vulnerable to the same disease. Pulling that lesson into our human world, I see the immeasurable value of different shapes, sizes, and ages; we cannot expect to sustain ourselves as a homogeneous breed of tall, thin, twenty-five year-olds. As I look at my body, and myself as a whole, I see great worth in my differences from others and my imperfection from the "ideal" dictated by mass society.

So, ironically, my time outdoors and love of nature have not made me less conscious of my body. But as I have spent more hours, days, months, and years in outdoor pursuits, I have abandoned the idea that my body needs to be thin. Instead, I have learned my body is MY tool, and by nurturing it, I can use it as I choose; instead, I have worked with women and men to reach common goals, and thereby gained a greater understanding of cooperation and competition; instead, I have looked at Mother Nature's design for living beings and seen that She pushes us to differ from one another, so that we can survive as a whole. I have seen the beauty and value of my body in its fortitude, its ability, but most of all, in itself.

Questions for Reflection

1. What relationship do you think existed between this author's high school athletic career and her body image development?

2. How does it feel for you to consider having a "fat layer" as a positive aspect of your body?

3. How do you think that participation in sports that include a focus on weight might impact the development of girls' body image in general?

MARATHON PRESENCE

Diane McManus

I passed from lens to lens, from eye to eye, keeping pace with my
appointment in Boston. I passed from e-mail to voice mail, from
heartbeat to heartbeat, friends and family greet
me with promises
of prayers, energy, and love.

Thursday the forecast promises rain, wind, cold, chilling
a dream, dampening spirits, aggravating PMS until aggravated assault
sounds attractive—but on whom or what? They're here for you. Ask.
Ask.
And before I can ask, there is the e-mail from Bonnie in Maine,
wishing me success and a happy
birthday, from Joan in Paris sending me energy and love, from Miriam
in Israel, saying good luck that day and every day.
And there is Shawn with a dove bar. There is Sandy, my running
partner, her energy and mine wrapping each other's
races. "I'll pray to the weather gods for you."
They brought presents and presence.

Friday came with a period ending a sentence
of crampy, bloated movement through the molasses morass of
mood.
And Saturday came, raining, but armed with a forecast of sun, I could
dream of light
hearts and steps. And Sunday came, wrapped
like a birthday gift in bright
ribbons of sky and clouds. It is easy
to forget
the chill of river air and sweat
that at twelve
miles will fill

flesh and bone. Yet remember then

they're here for you, your ancestors—your grandmother celebrates birth
hers and yours, giving her voice (keep going. You're almost halfway there. Yes,
You can make it.) Listen.

And here, running beside me, before me, ahead of me, behind me
voices. "You going for Boston?" "Go for it, girl! You're gonna do it."
"Go, Diane! All right Fast Tracks!"

Your family is here for you.
Watch. My sister Pat and the boys show up just after ten miles. "Yay, Diane!" Hugs.
Hug stops matter as much as water stops. Both are hug stops.
Both are water stops. Balance
restored, I am off. Welcomed into Pat's camera, then Dona's, then
startled at eighteen, "Diane, use your arms, concentrate! PR pace!"
Russell yells, scaring away
whatever slow was building up—
Surprised again at twenty by my name. "Come on, Diane!"
and here on a corner in Manayunk . . . Mom and brother Pete.
And Dona invested with the gift
of bilocation, back on Kelly Drive at the Falls Bridge,
bridging the distance between me and my dream. "Diane! You're doing great!"

If I can just keep running. . .
The runners are here for you. Don't forget them.
"Want some candy?"
Reaching into a bag, he hands me a hard candy. Reaching into their hearts, they cheer me, yell my
name.

I mumble prayers and run harder than my legs think is right. Your body is here for you. Thank her. "Qualify, qualify, qualify," I cry inside until the clock faces me with the news. You're in!

The spectators, the water givers, the masseuses, strangers, family,
friends, coaches, ancestors,
your God, your angels
are here for you. I listen
to the answering machine filled with voices of congratulations.
"Thoughts and prayers are with you," Richard says.
"You'll make Boston and come to see us." "Awesome race," Robin
says.
And from Paris
Joan calls for the news.

You are here for you. You listened. You did it.

Remember this when you reflect on the loneliness
of the long distance runner.

Questions for Reflection

1. What is the first thing you thought of as you finished reading this poem?

2. How do you think this author would describe her body?

3. What role has attaining physical goals played in the development of your body image?

4. How do you feel about the marathon running, triathlon and other endurance sports?

∫OLO

Ann Vilen

That summer my work in a university editorial office had become a slow suffocation. I sat at my desk behind the chic aqua partition separating my cubicle from my colleagues feeling small and angry. "∫ee Mary re.∫ept. deadline" wriggled behind a yellow push-pin on the bulletin board. I removed the pin and reinserted it forcefully between the "a" and the "r," practicing a bit of office voodoo. The clock rolled around to 4:00, when I was scheduled to see my therapist. I hung on to that appointment like a woman clinging to a raft. It had become a ritual as I drove the freeway to the therapist's office to think about death, about that long swim into a dark sea. Even the thought was a letting go. The image of bubbles streaming like luminous fish from the drowned victim's mouth prompted a barrage of shuddering tears.

"You're like a blowfish," the therapist once told me, "puffing yourself up to make yourself bigger, to ward off intruders. Why do you want to be alone?" Drawing her long legs up under her body into the chair, she waited for me to begin. My face was constantly working, but hers was a study of inquiry, always listening, jaw muscles and brow calm and smooth. ∫o I sometimes felt that my answers merely disappeared, like stones swallowed by a glassy pool. "You are choosing to be alone," she said flatly, the voice of a scientist observing some oddity under her microscope.

After therapy I usually swam laps at the campus pool. The even black lines on the bottom of the pool straightened my muddled thinking. I pulled myself along them methodically, as if the action of stroke, kick, breathe, stroke could keep my life on course. Occasionally a gasp of panic would force its way through the hush of my breathing as I made the U-turn at the end of the lane, and I would have to fight the urge to veer off into an oncoming swimmer. It wouldn't be as final as a highway accident, but it might annoy him enough to move over into another lane. Then I could have this one to myself. I could move at my own pace, stroke, kick, breathe, turn, push, kick, stroke, stroke, stroke, until I simply expired from the effort of it and collapsed into a lifeless, fetal question mark on the tile bottom.

On dry land, I had begun to pull my hair out. My husband didn't understand why I didn't crave sex the way he did. To boost my desire, he'd lavish my body with compliments: "I like your tight little unit," "I love it when you wear your hair down." But his compliments disgusted me, as if he were worshipping some image in a fun-house mirror. I couldn't name the loathing I felt or trace its roots down into what appeared publicly to be a conventional and successful work life and marriage. I simply felt consumed by rage, hating my life, desperate for a way out of the crowd whose gaze pinned me down like an insect in a collection labeled "powerless women."

One day toward the end of that summer I decided to get rid of the other swimmers dawdling in my lane for good. I decided to go backpacking alone in a wilderness area in Western North Carolina known for its rushing stream and deep swimming holes. There, I thought, I can finally have the water to myself. I had never been there before, nor had I ever backpacked alone (though I was an experienced woodswoman with dozens of group backpacking trips to my credit). But being alone, somewhere new without my husband, friends, or anyone else was the point. I needed to get away from all the splash. On my last lap, I rolled over onto my back, extended one arm toward the wall behind me, and submerged my face, staring up at the fluorescent ceiling lamps through the water. This must be what it looks like in those near death visions, I thought, the light diffused and beautiful and calling.

The next day I called in sick to work, told my husband I was going on a trip for the weekend, and packed my gear. Before the afternoon turned into dark I found a campsite well off the trail beside a small stream and set up my tent and supplies. This much was familiar, and my limbs moved easily through the tasks. Shortly after dusk, with a meal in my belly and a fire blazing, water for tea just coming to a boil, a man with a small white dog stumbled into my camp.

"Oh, sorry," he blurted, pushing his way through the underbrush. "I've gotten onto the wrong trail. I'm supposed to be on the main one, down to the river. It shouldn't be far."

"No, it's just over there," I explained. It was dark and I felt suddenly cut off by the stream and the steep hillside behind me. In my head, I heard the familiar slap of heels making a flip turn right behind me.

"Are you here alone?" he inquired. I felt my hackles rise, my eyes dart toward my tent, as if there were some safety there. But before I could decide whether to lie or tell the truth, he began a lengthy apology. "I didn't mean to scare you," he muttered. "Of course that was a nosy question. Thanks for the directions." He was on his way, his little dog prancing behind him.

As I watched him go, I felt both angry and afraid. What right did he have asking those questions? Would he return to attack me later? How could I at 105 pounds defend myself? I considered returning to the car and home at first light. As the night deepened and my fire died down, the woods closed in. The cicadas in the branches were too loud, ominous, a reminder that the forest is full of creatures—men as well as wild animals. I imagined footsteps down by the creek and puzzled over makeshift weapons—fuel from my stove, a heavy rock. The sounds, and the silence, seemed more deafening than when I had camped with someone else. It was like being at the bottom of a well, the woods damp and close and black, each noise echoing against the solid presence of the air itself. I thought about what my therapist had asked, and answered her. I want to be alone but also safe, with someone but not threatened. Perhaps it is security itself—alone or in numbers—that is an illusion.

In the morning I fixed myself a breakfast of salty instant soup and bannock, a flat fried bread. Letting the soup burn like wildfire down my throat, I reflected on how I had awakened in the night, startled from a dream I couldn't remember. It was pitch black. I had peered in what I thought must be the direction of the screen door, into the woods. But I could see nothing, not even the hand in front of my face. I thought I must be lost in that dark sea. Then I found the sky, still there, silent and speckled with light. Though vast, its palate seemed not so much to dwarf me as to envelope me, to hold me up and honor me. I reached out to the Seven Sisters and felt for the first time in months connected.

After breakfast I followed a path upstream along the bank till the path veered away from the river. I stayed with the water, boulder hopping along the creek. I came to a series of waterfalls and decided to make my way as best I could along the bank next to the falls. I had to climb up several crevices and worried about twisting an ankle or stumbling into the falls. I imagined the rescue team remarking over my mangled body about the stupidity of a woman hiking alone. "What was she thinking? This is no place for a woman, certainly not a petite, fragile novice. Cute though, isn't she? Wasn't she?" More than once I had to cross the river. I put my boots over my shoulder and went barefoot, curling my toes around the slippery rocks. It surprised me that I could walk knee deep through rushing water without losing my balance.

Finally, late in the morning I came to a stretch of water that ran smooth but fast about a foot deep over flat steps, falling five or six feet to each terrace. In several places, the water had gouged deep bowls into the rock of the river bottom, so that the current though quite swift on the surface, was still and slow in these deep pools. The richly mineraled rock swirled and deepened like sculpture beneath the current, giving the place the ambiance of something ancient and primitive.

Daring myself aloud, I left my clothes on the bank and waded out to the lip of a bowl about six feet in diameter; it was deep enough to swim. Naked and anxious, I plunged in and shimmied quickly across the pool. It was only a few seconds, but enough to convince me I wouldn't wash out into the current and over a falls just yards away. The second time I stayed in. Thrilling! Startling! Cold! Lying with my elbows propped on the rim of the bowl, my head back to catch the intensifying sun on my face and breasts, I marveled at how calm the water was in the rock pool. Around me the river rushed past to the next cascade. Suspended on a lily pad of sunlight, I let my body stream to the surface of the water and felt the ripening sensation of warm air against cool skin. The dappled greens and blues of trees and sky were dizzying. I remembered that scene in "Incident at Oxbow Bridge," where the soldier imagines that he has escaped his hanging—the rope shattered, the difficult swim under a rain of bullets, his chest heaving as he rolls over on the bank—and sees, perhaps for the first time, the infinitesimal grandeur of the natural world. All the while he is on the bridge, the noose tightening, the sky indifferent as his own executioner. Like him I noticed the leaves hanging translucent as paper chimes from slender twigs, sky the color of God's eyes, the sunlight tripping over the water like a skipping stone. And I too wished away the rope tightening around my life.

Afterward, I sat in my underwear on a sloping rock beside a roaring falls, reading poems aloud. "Shall we pitch ourselves into the terror? Shall we come home? Enter darkness, weep, know the dimension of absence, the unreachable deep" asks Susan Griffin in *Prayer for Continuation*. How appropriate these words seemed, as if written for me, for this place. Absorbed in the words on the page, a splash of white water caught the corner of my eye. I was suddenly disoriented, falling, spinning off the rock, my nails digging grooves into the lichen, the water's hands around my neck pulling me down. I lurched back for something solid and safe, landed hard with the small of my back against the jutting rock, my fingers tight around a rhododendron branch. It was all illusion, the feeling of falling into the brink that sent me instinctively diving for cover. I was safe on the rock, firmly anchored above the rushing water.

That night sitting by my fire with my camp around me, I was not afraid. I thought about why I had come—a longing for solitude, a need to escape my colleagues at the office, the gaze of my husband and a culture that defines women as dependent, small, powerless. In her journal *Three Summers*, Yvonne Pepin says, "I know women who accept the fact that they are physically weaker than men and ride through life as passive observers. They let themselves be carried by men over situations, never really demanding of their bodies, strengthening their dependence on men." That afternoon on the trail I had met a number of parties. Some included women, but the men did the talking. I recognized the pattern from my own hiking with Bill. The other parties were just men. I ran into the guy with the dog again. This time he just nodded and moved on. Two fishermen introduced themselves, asked "Where you from? Been out long?" I protected myself, deflected their intrusions by asking whether the fish were biting. When I had told a friend who called the night before I left home of my plans to backpack alone, she too had been afraid. "What does Bill think of it?" she asked. Why is it men's prerogative to confine and protect us? I did not ask Bill's permission. I did not want to know if he would worry. I needed the independence of doing this alone. I needed to know I could carry all of my own gear, set up my own camp, plan my own itinerary, and most difficult of all, enjoy my own company.

My last night out, I sat with my back against the muscled trunk of a beech tree. I recalled the arms of the river, sometimes a restful embrace, sometimes a vicious stranglehold. Always somehow human. Night deepened. The voices of cicadas and the stream rose like a chorus of women. The fire-light drew a circle of safety around my camp, like the globe of a lamp. And we sang together—the fire, the stars, the river, the insects, the breeze, the earth, and my pen swimming between the lines of my journal. I had gathered the greens of the forest, the blue-gray watercolors of the river into my nostrils all day. They smelled of fire and growth and rot. I knew with sudden finality —just as I had suddenly known the perfume of wild ginger after carrying the familiar, but elusive plant back to my camp —that I was neither lost, nor falling. Life rushes confusedly around me. My flailing at a culture that wants to define me as tiny and decorative and superficial exhausts and defeats me. But here in the wilderness, solo, I am strong and alive. I float in a still pool.

Questions for Reflection

1. What did the author hope to gain on her "solo?"

2. To what extent do you think she was successful?

3. How do you think the author feels about her body?

4. How do you feel her physical ability impacts her body image?

5. What experiences have you had that are similar to the author's?

Chapter III. Transforming

MOONLIGHT PADDLE

Jean Faulk

Paddling along mother earth's womb with the
Shimmering glow of the night star lighting the path,
My spirit is filled with the warm peace of the closing day.

As the moon drifts behind a lingering cloud,
My eyes no longer see the way and my other senses are heightened
My lips and tongue embrace the flavor of the evening breeze
My ears reach out to sense each nearby rustle on the riverbank
My nostrils can almost smell the earth cooling in the rising dew
And my skin swells to encompass the void and touch the stars.

As the cloud passes and the light returns, I regain my human form
But a sprinkling of dust from the universe has attached itself to my
soul
And I see more than the path.

Questions for Reflection

1. What strikes you most about this piece?

2. What do you think wilderness and "seeing" mean to this author in terms of body image?

3. What do they mean to you?

A JOURNEY OF TRANSFORMATION

Mary McClintock

I used to hate mirrors. Now I seek them out. I used to hate having my picture taken and seeing pictures of myself. Now I take pictures of myself and have ten pictures of me on my bedroom wall. I used to avoid bright-colored, form-fitting, body-hugging clothes. Now I revel in them. I used to hate how my body felt when I exercised, sweating and breathing hard. Now I crave those feelings.

Basically, I used to hate my body— it's size, shape and limitations. Since I was nine years old, throughout my growing up, my mother, sister and I were on constant diets. I grew to believe the teasing I got about being fat and ugly. Now I love the way I feel and look and all that my body can do. When I try to explain the transformations of the last year to my friends, they all ask, what happened? It's been a long and complex journey, but my answer is quite simple: a series of sea kayak trips and turning forty. Sex and the love of marvelous women also had a big part in my journey, but that is another story for another anthology.

I've sea kayaked for thirteen years, but had never done a long trip. For years, I'd dreamt of a long kayak trip, one where I could keep going around the next point to explore where the land meets the sea. Somehow, I always knew that if I could just be out on a trip long enough I'd be able to get in shape. I've always avoided anything that seemed like regular "exercise." I wouldn't consider doing something that even approached "working out." But being on a long trip would be different. Maybe I could build strength and endurance without really noticing. And it would be a lot more fun.

Twenty years ago, I tried to do a longer trip, actually a series of long trips: mountaineering, climbing, caving and cross country skiing for a semester in the Rockies through the National Outdoor Leadership School (NOLS). But carrying a sixty-five pound pack was more than my body could handle. One week into the course, the day after my twenty-first birthday, I lost my balance crossing a boulder field and dislocated my kneecap. I was evacuated after only ten days in the mountains and never returned to complete the course.

I've spent a lot of time outdoors since the NOLS course, both working as an outdoor leader and on my own trips with friends. But I never was out on a trip for more than ten days. Life and work and my own self-limitations kept me from heading out for my long dream trip. I kept finding reasons to limit myself to less challenging, shorter trips.

At some point, a few years ago, I decided that life was too short to stay in stressful, dissatisfying jobs and to not pursue my dream of a long trip. The prospect of turning forty clinched it. I decided that I would do a long trip before I turned forty.

At first, I planned to go to Newfoundland, a place that promised lots of challenging paddling and wild country, yet was still accessible by car from my home in Massachusetts. I could take my own kayak and not have to pay for a plane ticket or kayak rental.

Then my friend Anne called. She was going to be in New Zealand on her way back from working at the South Pole. She said the sea kayaking possibilities in New Zealand were endless and asked me to join her there for some paddling. It was a much bolder and more expensive trip than Newfoundland, but I pretty quickly decided that it truly would be a dream-of-a-lifetime trip. Deciding to make the trip to New Zealand happen was a major shift for me. It was a step toward choosing myself in a way I'd never done before and toward a journey of transformation in how I felt about my body.

Anne and I talked at length about the kind of trip we wanted. I wanted to kayak for at least three weeks, but not do a grueling, long mileage expedition. I wanted time to explore and power-lounge and be wind-bound without being worried about making a particular destination. I was a bit concerned that my loungeful paddling style would feel boring or unchallenging to Anne, who I thought of as being a very energetic, gung-ho, adventurous outdoorswoman. After all, she'd done long trips as a NOLS and Outward Bound instructor and had skied across Greenland and Antarctica as part of the American Women's Antarctic Expedition. How would she feel about a relaxed trip? I'd had problems once with a friend who thought my style and pace of paddling were irritatingly low-key.

But Anne was agreeable to a more relaxed trip. In fact, she looked forward to having time to learn about the local natural history and to bake bread and other goodies with her Pam Banks Fry-Bake pan. She even said she was nervous about whether I was going to be too gung-ho for her, since I had lots more sea kayaking experience than she did.

The Marlborough Sounds trip was a joy. Anne and I were perfect trip companions, falling into an easy rhythm of paddling, exploring, lounging, and camp chores. And we were very well matched as paddling partners. We had agreed to start slowly and not cover a lot of miles at the beginning of the trip when both of us would be out of shape from not paddling and when our boats would be heaviest with food and gear. Actually, I felt like I had to restrain myself at first from wanting to paddle up around the next point, explore further.

Just as I thought it might be, the process of getting in better physical shape on the trip was gradual and barely noticeable. It felt wonderful and natural to be living outdoors, using my body in all the daily camping chores of hauling gear and boats up and down beaches, paddling, and hiking.

I continued to be pretty unconscious about my body until the day we hiked up the Nydia Track to the Nydia Saddle. For years, I've avoided hiking, preferring instead to go for what I call strolls. A large part of this had been my desire to avoid hurting my knees, which have been problematic since the injury on the NOLS course twenty years ago. For years, carrying any real pack weight and hiking up and down steep trails had meant a great deal of pain in my joints.

Deciding to hike up the relatively steep trail to Nydia Saddle was a departure from my norm. All my worries about "keeping up" with Anne, the strong expedition member, came back. I also was nervous about keeping my balance on slippery, rocky stream crossings. Anne was great, encouraging me in a gentle way and modeling that it was okay to sweat and get short of breath.

For years, I'd avoided hiking that meant either sweating or panting. I felt embarrassed by my body's tendency to sweat profusely during what seemed to be very little exercise. And I didn't like the feeling of getting out of breath.

So, there I was hiking and sweating and panting. . .and feeling okay about it. Anne didn't seem to think I was a wimp or hate me for my panting and sweating. And the views were gorgeous, the wildlife and plants fascinating. I was very glad I'd pushed myself to sweat and pant my way up the hill. We went for two other hikes around the bay while we were windbound in Nydia Bay. And I began to really enjoy the feel of my leg muscles moving and stretching, especially my thigh muscles.

I didn't really notice my growing upper body strength and confidence in my paddling skills until we faced the two roughest stretches of water during the last week of the trip. The paddle from Torea Bay out around Pihaka Point to Kaipakirikiri was the roughest water we'd paddled. It was the first time I'd been in wind so strong that I thought the paddle was going to be blown out of my hands. I was scared, but I dug hard into the water with each stroke and my boat responded, staying upright in the building waves. When we got into calmer water I felt relieved and proud that we'd managed such difficult conditions.

The paddle across the end of Resolution Bay was the shortest paddle of the trip, but also the roughest. A strong southerly wind had blown up in a very short period of time and what had been calm water was transformed into large waves and crashing surf. We had to launch into big surf, the first time I'd ever done that, and paddle at a ferry angle across the waves. Again, the wind was strong enough to feel like it would pull the paddle out of my hands. I gripped the paddle tightly and used every muscle in my body to paddle into and across the waves. I focused on meeting each wave at an angle that would both maximize my forward movement and keep the boat from tipping over. When we finally reached our destination, my shoulders and arms were exhausted and sore. I knew that I wouldn't have been able to handle such conditions at the beginning of the trip. I had gotten stronger.

I hadn't realized my upper body wasn't the only part of me getting stronger. By bracing and using my whole body with each stroke, I was also building strong leg muscles. Their strength became apparent when we hiked from Resolution Bay to Ship Cove and back on the next to last day of the trip. It was only a week after the Nydia Saddle hike, yet I felt completely different. My legs felt great. I loved the feel of the nylon swishing on my quads as I hiked up steep sections of the trail. My thighs and calves felt strong and sturdy. And my knees didn't hurt. I think strengthening my quads really helped support my knees. As we hiked down a very steep section of trail, I joked with Anne about how I was going to really whine when we had to hike back up that section. But on the way back, I went right by it without even noticing the steepness. I was too busy being thrilled with the feel of my powerful thigh muscles.

Coming home from New Zealand was very hard for many reasons. It was hard to figure out what was next after living such a long-held dream. I knew that somehow I had to hold on to and build on how I was beginning to feel about my body. I felt more alive and present in my body than I'd ever felt before and I was desperate to not lose that feeling.

I was determined to get outside as much as I could, especially paddling. And I knew I needed support to sort out my feelings about myself and my body. In the early 80's, I'd done a combination of emotional therapy and body-work with a woman named Linda Tumbarello. I decided I wanted to work with her again. She does something called Body-Mind Centering® that involves movement, breathing and increased body awareness. A lot of what she does is geared towards developing greater awareness of different parts of the body and how they're connected, offering the possibility of shifting movement from stiff, seized-up motions to more articulated, fluid movements.

My work with Linda was an essential part of my transformation to loving myself and my body. The combination of dealing with emotional issues and healing from a lifetime of hating my body and of exploring new ways of moving and feeling has been very freeing.

The work with Linda helped my adjustment to being home. After the initial culture shock of my return from New Zealand, I faced the question of what my next dream was. I'd lived a dream I'd had for twenty years. What was next? One thing I decided very quickly was that I wasn't going to wait another twenty years to do a trip that was longer than a week. My goal is to do a longer kayak trip every year. And I decided that I wanted to work toward a more energetic, expedition-like trip. Not something huge and dramatic, but something that was somehow more challenging, longer mileage, more difficult paddling conditions. I found that what I wanted was to push myself more. What I really wanted to do was a trip to Prince William Sound in Alaska....a trip I'd fantasized about since college.

Thinking far ahead was hard at that time, but I knew that the way to make a dream happen was to build toward it every day. And what I needed to make a trip like Prince William Sound happen was to be stronger and to develop more skills. So I started paddling a lot, almost every day. And instead of loungeful paddling, I did more of what I now call workout paddles.

I live 15 minutes from a lovely section of the Connecticut River. I began a routine of paddling my sea kayak upstream on the river and then back down. I paddled anywhere from 20 minutes to an hour every day. The river conditions varied, sometimes there was a lot of current and wind, sometimes very little. I paddled hard upstream against the current, pushing myself until I was sweaty and out of breath. Instead of wanting to avoid such exertion, I now craved it. I was thrilled with the feeling of my muscles working hard and the movement of my whole body as I paddled. There were wonderful moments of feeling the push and pull of a stroke as it moved from my bracing feet, up through my calves and powerful thighs, through my hips and torso to my shoulders, arms and hands. At one point, I realized that I was moving fluidly, more fluidly than I'd ever remembered moving.

I got stronger and built up my muscles through those daily workout paddles. And I also developed an addiction to the way I felt during and after the workouts. I was definitely producing lots of endorphins with all that exertion. And the calming feel of the endorphins was great. I'd start out a paddle with my brain and heart racing with thoughts and emotions, and by the end of the paddle, my heart and brain were calm, and I felt alive and refreshed. I grew to crave my daily paddles, feeling edgy if I didn't get out for some form of exercise.

Part of the joy of those workout paddles was the sheer delight of being outdoors on a beautiful section of river. I thought I would get bored seeing the same stretch of river everyday. But I never did. Everyday the light and sky were different, the water levels and current varied with rain and drought and dam releases. And the wildlife varied from red-tailed hawks, ospreys, bald eagles and great blue herons to swimming raccoons and browsing deer. Being outside and feeling connected to the wild was another essential part of the transformation of how I felt about myself and my body.

Just as with the New Zealand trip, the change in my body through the months of my workout paddles was a gradual one that I didn't notice as it was happening. Several experiences really brought home to me how my body and attitudes had been transformed.

Some of those experiences were kayak trips on the coast of Maine in the months after my return from New Zealand. I had decided that along with building strength through more paddling, I wanted to build my skills and confidence by paddling in more challenging conditions. This required a mental adjustment from my worries and insecurities of the past. A several-day trip in Maine with my friends, Karen and Angel, provided some valuable lessons about trusting myself and my abilities. I had told them I wanted to push myself to paddle more challenging water, and they were game. But when it was already quite breezy at six in the morning and we were headed out towards more exposed water that might be windier, I started to express my anxiety about the conditions we might face. Karen stopped me and said, "Mary, you can't worry about what the conditions are going to be like this afternoon. You just have to paddle the water that's in front of you." That stopped me in my tracks. I realized I'd spent a lot of time worrying about the "rough water" that lay ahead and not paying attention to what was right in front of me. Thinking back to the Marlborough Sounds trip, I realized that was what had gotten me through those two very rough paddles. Being present in the moment and focusing on the wave that was right in front of me was what I needed to do both in paddling and in my life.

For the rest of the trip with Karen and Angel, if I focused on the next wave, I did fine, even in conditions that a few months before would have freaked me out. The type of conditions that have always been scariest for me are following seas, waves from behind that lift the kayak and push it forward into a surfing action. By the end of the trip with Karen and Angel, when we hit a section of such surfing waves, I found that instead of being afraid, I was having fun! I focused on each wave, working at catching it at just the right angle for the longest ride. When we got through that section of water, I even wanted to go back and do it again. Karen laughed at how much I'd changed just on that one trip.

I knew I felt different, and that my body shape and size and appearance had changed with all the paddling I had been doing. But I'd avoided thinking about the fact that I was losing weight. I wanted to focus on how great I felt and not get into evaluating myself based on my weight loss. I had grown up with a daily obsession about dieting and weight and had been trained to the attitude that losing weight means you're a good person, and gaining weight means you're bad. I wanted the way I felt about myself to be related to how my body felt, not to how many pounds I weighed. So when people asked about whether I'd lost weight, I said, "yeah, I guess so, mostly I think I'm building muscles."

Then I saw my friend, Laurie, for the first time in several months and I couldn't avoid her stunned look. She said, "what happened to you? You look great!" I explained about paddling and she was amazed at the transformation. She knew that I used to spend more time drifting in my kayak than pushing hard.

I asked if she wanted to join me for one of my workout paddles. This felt pretty bold as Laurie is an athlete, an accomplished whitewater canoeist and cross-country skier. She'd just returned from a five-week climbing trip and was in great shape. We'd sea kayaked together on several trips, but always with the understanding that we would go at my more low-key pace. I've always looked up to her as being very fit and highly skilled.

When we started out from the launching spot, Laurie immediately commented on the force of the current as we paddled upstream. I said it felt about average for that stretch of river. We paddled hard and chatted away, catching up on the news of the past few months.

Several more times, Laurie commented on the strength of the current. We stopped talking where the water is constricted between an island and the shore and the current becomes even more powerful. Once up and around the island, as we drifted downstream, Laurie said, "You really have changed. You would never have pushed yourself that way before." I started thinking about all that I'd been doing and looked at Laurie paddling along in her sleek boat and looked at myself and my boat and thought, "Wow, maybe I'm really becoming more of a peer of Laurie's. Maybe I'm even becoming an "athlete." It was a powerful and exciting realization.

Laurie's comment that I looked like I'd lost weight, and the inescapable fact that my clothes were beginning to feel uncomfortably baggy, made me decide to weigh myself. I was shocked to find that I'd lost about 35 pounds since I'd left for the trip to New Zealand. I was stunned. I hadn't been trying to lose weight. But my body had really changed. Although how I feel about my body is an ongoing evolution, the culmination of my transformation felt like it happened on the three-day solo kayak trip in Maine that I took on my actual fortieth birthday. New Zealand had been a celebration of turning forty, but it actually happened about six months before my birthday.

Mary in her kayak

For my birthday trip I headed out by myself, determined to paddle further out in Muscongus Bay, Maine than I'd gone before. It was a tough paddle, made even more so by near zero visibility fog and landing in crashing surf. After a very challenging first 24 hours of the trip, I decided to treat myself to a more restful time on Black Island, my favorite island on the coast.

As I sat in my favorite lounging area in the shade, looking out on the breezy sunlit bay, I was truly happy. I decided to stroll around the island to some gorgeous rock formations, thinking the light would be good for pictures. Over the past six weeks, I'd started taking pictures of myself with the remote control feature of my camera. I'd decided I wanted pictures of my "new" body, and felt most comfortable taking pictures of myself rather than having someone else take them. I'd even taken a series of pictures of myself in my bold new magenta Lycra shorts that I wore on my workout paddles.

I had on the magenta shorts and a T-shirt as I wandered around on the slabs of rocks. Seeing a big boulder, I thought that it would be a great place to prop my camera for using the remote control. So I did. I remembered what Anne had said after seeing the picture I'd taken of myself on an earlier trip. She said it looked great, but that it would be interesting to take pictures of myself in other than my usual poses.

I tried to figure out different poses. I laughed out loud at myself, a newly forty-year-old woman, flexing her muscles for her camera in the breeze on a sunny island off the coast of Maine. And then I remembered beautiful pictures I'd seen of naked women stretched out on curved slabs of granite. I looked down at my floppy T-shirt and decided it had to go. I took pictures of myself stretched out on the rock in just my magenta shorts. I was both thrilled and amazed at how great I felt, how in love with myself I felt. Never in my wildest dreams would I have imagined that I'd spend my fortieth birthday cavorting around on rocks in the sun, taking pictures of myself and loving myself.

Questions for Reflection

1. What do you think were the most important factors that helped the author make her "journey of transformation?"

2. How do these factors relate to traditional diet mentality vs. a non-diet mentality?

3. Which, if any, of these factors do you recognize in your own journey?

BODY

Donna Glee Williams

For this gift, it is my fathers I must thank
My mothers' bodies were stolen long ago
hobbled and broken
manacled and bent and
stolen

My fathers were my teachers
(my mothers were dead)
flexing and sweating against the rock
lifting the load onto brown shoulders
skipping like goats from rock to rock
while my mothers' white eyes
stared at the walls of their coffins

I chopped the lid for firewood
and now my coffin is a boat
rowed strong against the stream
we make our slow triumphant way

My shoulders may not be man-broad
but I lift the load

I may climb cautiously over the rocks
one hand to steady me

But in my other hand
I have my ax
and daughter
no one will steal your body
while I live.

Questions for Reflection

1. What are you feeling and thinking as you read this author's words?

2. What might "mothering" have to do with body image development in this piece?

3. What do you think of fathers as role models for daughters in the development of healthy body image?

SOARING

Karla A. Henderson

I'd been eyeing the 25-foot platform all morning on that perfect July day in Alaska. The temperatures hovered at 65 degrees with a sunny blue sky sprinkled with wispy high ice clouds. Every time I looked at that high perch, my heart rate sped. I had had a good week as a visiting faculty member doing classroom teaching about adventure education and its value in schools and recreation programs. We'd now moved into the experiential aspects of the course. My co-leader was an expert regarding the practical side of adventure education, and we were hoping the students would get a chance today to encounter how ropes courses worked. We were trying various challenge activities to build cooperation and teamwork in our group with the afternoon devoted to the high ropes course.

Although I love the outdoors and challenge activities, most of my interest has been with research and theory. In my teaching, I always found someone else who could lead adventure activities such as climbing, rappelling, and the low or high ropes course. I hadn't done any of the high elements of a ropes course for years. Since today's class was small and Todd was the group leader, I thought my role now was as a cheerleader. That platform, however, continued to seduce me.

The "pamper pole," the name given to the platform, was to be the climax of the activities of the day. I don't know why they call it a pamper pole. The activity requires trusting one's equipment with lots of mental courage. Once a person gets to the top of the platform on the pole, the goal is to jump out and grab hold of a trapeze several feet away. If you catch it, you get to swing out of it. If you miss, you fall but only for a split second before the belay device and harness system catches you to be lowered gently to the ground.

One of the confident males volunteered to go first. He was hooked into a chest harness system with a double rope attached from above to the rigging. The other end of the rope was attached to a belayer who was strapped to a pole so that he was immovable. The system offered virtually no possibility of any kind of injury unless the bindings weren't fitted or connected properly. This system was standard for everyone who wanted to go onto the pamper platform and the leader checked and double-checked it before anyone ascends the pole. Kevin boldly climbed the pole using the ladder system until he was 25 feet in the air perched on a two foot by two foot platform. Standing on the platform alone is difficult because the platform wobbles in the wind as high branches do in trees. He leaped through the air towards the trapeze suspended eight feet away and missed it. The belay system held him, and Todd lowered him to the ground.

Larry went next. He wasn't quite as confident, but his 6'5" frame enabled him to grab the trapeze somewhat effortlessly even though he hesitated briefly before he jumped. It was now someone else's turn. Larry teased as he was lowered down, "It's your turn Karla." I just smiled.

Barb said to me, "I'll go if you'll go."

I wanted to try it, but I also was afraid of getting up there and then not being able to jump. I've always been pretty comfortable with my body, but at 46 years old, I didn't want to push it either. My middle age body was in pretty good shape and I wanted to keep it that way. I didn't want to be a chicken, but I also didn't want to fail. Now I knew better what students felt like who were in my classes. A metaphor about letting go of the shore to get across the river ran through my mind. That metaphor was appropriate then for my personal life. I wanted to try new things but I was often afraid of letting go. I struggled for what felt like hours in my mind. Should I? Shouldn't I? I'm scared. It's perfectly safe. What if I get up there and can't do it? What if I freeze? My body might be willing, but what if my mind won't? What will the students think if I don't jump? What does it feel like to do the pamper pole? If I don't do it today, will I ever have another chance? I hesitated for a moment and then said, "OK." Barb gave a nervous laugh. She really didn't think that I would try the jump, and she knew that I wouldn't let her go back on her challenging quip.

I donned the harness. I've never been glad I was so flat chested, but it has its positive dimensions when it comes to these straps of webbing across one's torso. They fit comfortably snug and I felt cradled in their security. Todd explained the belay system as he checked and double-checked the gear and hooked both of us into the safety system. I was now committed to this adventure despite many second thoughts.

After years of teaching about the value of these activities, my rational side knew that no matter what, I was physically safe. That didn't stop my knees from shaking. My heart was pounding so hard I was afraid it was going to loosen the safety straps around my chest. I looked at the top of the pole from the ground level one last time, took a deep breath, and walked over to the base of the shaft. I couldn't think about it any longer. I reached my hand to the closest rung of the ladder secured against the pole and began the climb. Hand over hand and foot over foot, I concentrated completely on my climbing. I didn't look up and I didn't look down until I reached the platform. Getting from the ladder onto the platform was a challenge I hadn't anticipated. Every muscle tightened as the pole swayed slightly. I finally inched my upper body over the platform, swung my legs around, and sat on the perch dangling my legs. I roosted for a moment waiting for my heart to slow down.

In a few seconds I began to look around. The Chugach Mountains were clearly visible in the east and I could just barely site the Alaskan range to the north. It was hazy or otherwise I might have been able to see Mt. McKinley in Denali National Park. The wooden fence surrounding the ropes course kept me from seeing these mountains when I was down below. Taking a deep breath, I felt as if I was on top of the world. At least what had happened so far was worth this amazing view. Then I looked down—all the way to the ground. I saw eight eager faces looking up at me. Barb called, "What's it look like up there?" Todd called out, "You look like you belong there-why don't you stand?"

"I will in a minute," I said. I was just trying to savor the moment or procrastinate—probably a little of both. "This feels funny being the center of attention with all you folks looking up at me."

"You've been the center of attention plenty of times before. I've seen you speak to hundreds of people and you don't seem to mind that attention," Todd said.

"Yeah, but that's different." I thought to myself, that's really different. Standing in front of people giving a speech doesn't require me to fling my body through the air.

I pulled my knees under me and gradually raised on to my feet facing the trapeze. I took a few more deep breaths. All the eyes were still on me when I glanced down quickly. I looked at the trapeze hanging a thousand miles away at about my eye level. I thought to myself, "I'm too short, I can never reach that." I'm average height and have a somewhat athletic frame but as much as I wanted to be successful, I could not envision my body stretching out to do this feat.

I scanned the horizon one more time thinking how beautiful the landscape was and how good the sun felt on my shoulders. I knew the more I thought about it, the less likely I was to jump. Yet, I was enjoying this feeling of satisfaction and uncertainty. I was glad to be there, but I couldn't stay. I needed to be lowered down so someone else could have a chance, or I needed to take a deep breath, count to three, and leap.

As I jumped and left the precarious security of the landing, I felt time stand still. I had the sensation of soaring as the trapeze got closer. I was going to have no problem grasping it. My hands hit the cold bar but my fingers didn't close on it fast enough. My palms slipped off the surface. I was surprised that I got so close, and then

Karla's smile

surprised again that I missed the clutch. In a split second I felt the pressure around my chest as the harness jerked me to a stop. Dangling by the rope, I yelled, "Wow!" I had jumped, sailed, almost reached the bar, and could still see the mountains in the distance.

As Todd gently lowered me to the ground, the group cheered. All I could do was smile. Now it was Barb's turn.

Questions for Reflection

1. Was the author's attempt successful?

2. How do you think this author feels about her physical self?

3. What does it feel like when you allow yourself to trust your body?

CLIMBER GIRL

∫usan Fox Rogers

The summer I spent in Tuolomne Meadows with Jonathan Bradley created a dividing line in my life, the before and after shots remarkably different. In the before shot a 120-pound girl with shoulder-length brown hair, round shoulders and thick muscle-bound thighs stares boldly at the world with green eyes that scrunch up, nearly closed by a smile that stretches past white teeth. It's hard to see anything but happiness there. In the after shot, round cheeks give way to distinct high cheekbones framed by short hair. Angular shoulder bones protrude from a tank top that hangs in ripples like a window curtain, loose and undefined. Eyes stare out past the camera, at something in the distance.

The few times I've told the story of that summer, my climbing friends fidget with envy. It's the trip they all wish they had taken when they were nineteen and had no cares in the world. But I don't talk much about that summer since tales of good trips sound like bragging. Yet the source of my silence is more complicated: I don't want my friends to know that what I loved most almost killed me. I don't want to sound overly dramatic, because this story isn't. It's flaw is that it's too common; it's a story of love and a story I share with too many girls.

Jonathan's offer came in March, during the second semester of my first year at Colorado College. I'd had crushes in high school, but never had I fallen so hard and fast as I did for Jonathan. I'd met him the summer before while climbing in Boulder. Tall and lanky, he appeared fearless on the rock. To me, he was climbing. Around him, I saw myself doing dumb things, twisting myself into the person I thought Jonathan would love, hanging on his every desire, need, whim. I climbed harder to awe him; I belayed him for hours marveling over every ridiculous impossible move he made on those vertical scary rock faces. My emotional acrobatics far surpassed anything on the rock, but oddly, no one was applauding.

Most of my first semester I'd spent waiting in my bare, cement-block dorm room every Friday night hoping Jonathan might call. He didn't. Spring semester I made myself busy. I was not going to be one of those pathetic girls who pine for boys who don't care. So he was lucky to find me when he called: I had three jobs, my class-work, and I climbed every day in the Garden of the Gods. Surprised to hear his voice on the phone line, I forgot my sadness that had turned to anger.

"Have you been climbing?" I asked. I wanted to boast about the routes I had done, hard leads on that red sandstone rock. I wanted him to be impressed.

"Not much," he said. "Cole and his girlfriend are going to spend the summer in Tuolomne," he said. "Want to go?" So casual, it almost wasn't a question.

"Yes," spilled out without reflection. But even as I said it, I knew I had been invited because this was a boys-with-their-girlfriends trip; if Cole had a girlfriend then Jonathan had to have one too. In the landscape of women climbers I was a pretty good pick: I didn't whine much, I didn't act like a girl. But my role on this trip was clear: girlfriend. And to climb with Jonathan, was worth it all.

Jonathan called again in early May. "Cole's female type left him," he said.

What I heard: the trip is off.

"He wants to spend the summer in Boulder feeling sorry for himself."

I remained silent for a long heartbeat. We had been counting on Cole's car for the trip. "Women," I said, "I mean female types."

"We can hitchhike," he said.

My heart raced. Already my parents were dubious about this trip, not so much about the climbing, but about the company. I'd have to tell a few lies.

"Yeh, we can hitchhike," I said.

We sealed our commitment to this trip by making love for the first time.

We left mid-June. Vedauwoo, Wyoming, just outside of Laramie, was our first stop. Located in the Medicine Bow National Forest, Vedauwoo looked, at a distance, like a pile of enormous boulders dumped from heaven. Between boulder jumbles stood conifers, straight sentinels, guarding the sky. Vedauwoo smelled of open land, hard rock, and the real West, a place where prisons once held outlaws like Butch Cassidy.

Under skies so clear they were white, we tiptoed on thin face holds, and jammed our taped-up fists into rough cracks. The sun beat down on our bare legs soon scratched bloody from the rough rock. At night, we retreated under a slab of rock, an enormous flat boulder. This became our house, and we joked about wanting windows and a front door. Jonathan promised to talk to the landlord. But until then, the wind swept through at night as we hunkered over our campstove, creating simple meals, macaroni and cheese or noodles plain with butter.

The one night Jonathan took over cooking, a pan of fried carrots appeared. Not convinced that carrots constituted a meal, I remained quiet, taking my cues from Jonathan: he wasn't interested in food, had lived for years off beer and cigarettes. If I wanted to climb hard I needed to forget I loved to eat.

While in Vedauwoo, we spent a lot of time hiking out to Reynold's Hill to work on a climb called Penis Dimension. I laughed at the name, sex and climbing overlapping so mysteriously, like life and climbing, like Jonathan and the rock. But the moment the thirty foot high piece of rock appeared in the horizon, I knew it was senseless to even try. I hated jam cracks, the way they swallowed my fists, chewed the skin from my knuckles. And this one overhung from top to bottom. I stood for hours holding the end of Jonathan's rope, urging him on, as he went up and down, up and down.

In the world of climbing, the belayer is the wife. She's the one who holds the rope, to catch her husband if he falls. But her real role is to stay secure on the ground or on a ledge, encouraging, letting out rope when needed, taking it in when yelled at. Her motions are all in response to his motions; she has to watch, to pay attention, to react. She does this because she loves him, wants to keep him safe.

When I climb, I watch, too, for holds, the next ledge, where it will get hard, where I might fall. I respond to the dips in the rock by throwing out a hip, or leaning my weight into the rock. I respond, as in a dance, the rock leading me around the dance floor. I do this because I love the rock.

That three-day stop over in Vedauwoo was a warm-up for the long hard climbs to come, but also for our relationship. Jonathan led the real climbs, the hard climbs, and I followed. At night, I cooked. I was the girlfriend, knew without learning how to do this. Our daily motions appeared compatible, our movement over rock efficient, an exterior harmony.

Yet at night when I settled into my sleeping bag, muscles pressed into the hard ground, I sensed something missing. I never reached out to touch him, afraid that was not what he wanted. His silence was that of the rocks, something I admired and feared. But it swallowed me at night when our movement stopped, when we were just two bodies cocooned in our sleeping bags. Lying still, I felt something closing inside of me, like the windows we didn't have on this outdoor house sliding shut.

Then, I couldn't see how that silence moved into me. But now I can trace its path, how, left without words, I began to use my body to speak. Movement on the rock spelled out my joy and worry. Jonathan's touch translated to hope. So hungry for that touch my body became hunger. I spoke the language of thinness. Only then neither Jonathan nor I could understand what I was saying.

***

Our rides to Tuolomne were mostly straightforward hauls with truckers who liked to talk. One spun a tale about a pal who transported cows. The winter before, a string of sub-zero temperatures left the cows frozen to the truck bed. He broke their legs to get them off the truck. I laughed at that story, out of horror or perhaps because I didn't believe it. But I also laughed because the trucker was laughing, his big belly rocking with the rhythm of the moving truck. And Jonathan was laughing too, his mouth open wide, head tossed back.

Out of Las Vegas, a black man in neat-pressed jeans picked us up. His thin arms grasped the steering wheel of the truck, and his forearms flexed, revealing sinewy muscles beneath a thin layer of skin. I crawled into the trucker's sleeping berth and dozed. Jonathan's head bobbed, snapped forward and back; he could barely remain awake after thirty hours of traveling. But this trucker wanted to talk. He punctuated his endless stream of stories with "Can you believe that?" I paid close attention as he detailed the long list of Christmas gifts he'd bought for his wife. It included a fur coat and a new microwave, two things I knew I'd always live without. But for a moment I wanted them.

"And she still wasn't happy," he declared thumping the enormous steering wheel. "What does it take to make a woman happy?"

"You're asking the wrong guy," Jonathan said.

I lay back in the sleeping berth, holding my breath. What makes me happy?

At 9,000 feet, Tuolomne Meadows sits high in the eastern part of Yosemite National Park. It was here that John Muir and Robert Underwood conceived of establishing the park. It's no wonder: the wide-open meadows dotted by granite domes that look like enormous grey babies' bottoms made me want to sing. Through this landscape of trimmed light-green grass and alpine ponds runs the Tuolomne River, narrow and cold. Tall pine trees ring the higher peaks that remain covered in snow well into the summer. The gentle appearance of the landscape is deceptive. The sides of those domes that had been cleaved off as if by a machete from heaven testify to a tumultuous geologic past and a dangerous present. This isn't country that people belong in for most of the year. Route 121 into Tuolomne from Lee Vining in the East crosses Tioga Pass and is closed from November until April. As the road through the pass narrowed and became steeper, the air thinned. At the crest of the hill we had a view of the Meadows below us, stretching wide with those domes, silently waiting.

Though Yosemite Valley with its enormous walls and El Capitan and Half Dome was a mecca for rock climbers, I was more interested in Tuolomne. There, it was 15-20 degrees cooler, less touristed, and in 1981 only a handful of climbers took up residence in the summertime. The climbing in both areas was challenging, but for different reasons. The Valley boasted long strenuous cracks, while Tuolomne was a feast for face climbers: those granite boulders, worn so smooth by wind and snow, offered only wrinkles, holds that varied from a ruler's width to the thickness of a dime. The occasional crack ran like a shot through the smooth side of these boulders, as if they had been dropped and snapped on impact. In those cracks Jonathan placed gear, the solid hexes and aluminum stoppers that would protect his falls. But most routes ran the edges of dark watermarks or the worn indentations of wind and rain, straight up the rock. Bolts, drilled into the rock and left by previous climbers, provided the best most secure protection. But the distance between bolts often spanned twenty feet. Or that's what we'd heard from fellow climbers, their eyes popping in exaggerated post-climb fear. We laughed as our palms sweated, our minds unconsciously calculating how that translated to forty-foot falls, or more. It was clear that climbing in the Meadows meant two things: you had to have a mind- and balls of steel. And you couldn't fall.

Our days in Tuolomne were deliciously routine. We set up our green Eureka Timberline in an area reserved for tents. On one side stood pine trees, then woods that trailed off into the wilderness. On the other side, RVs and their hookups, near to the small stone building that housed toilets and sinks for washing dishes. Our Compacted soil marked off our plot and a wooden picnic table served as living room. We kept our food-peanut butter, noodles, cans of tomato sauce-in a large blue stuff sack suspended from a nearby pine tree. Black bear regularly entered tents and cars, taking anything edible. A ranger explained that even hanging food didn't work anymore. They called them kamikaze bears, the ones who climbed trees then launched into the air, landing on the food sacks, and bringing it all to the ground. I delighted in those kamikaze bears and their unstoppable desires. When finally one day they did get our food, I marveled at the way they had unscrewed the jar of peanut butter and licked it clean. Everything was gone except the coffee. This was good, because more and more we lived on caffeine and adrenaline.

Breakfast was almost always coffee and eggs over easy. Then, rope draped over my shoulder, gear hanging from Jonathan's side, we'd head out. "Another day, another climb," Jonathan said as we walked toward the two-lane road for our morning commute. I'd stick out my thumb. We never waited long. Families, Winnebagos traveling through national parks, mothers exploring alone with their children stopped for us. They'd all say: we don't usually pick up hitchhikers. But before we were dropped off, often a short drive down the road, I was exchanging addresses, telling these instant friends to stop if they made it to Colorado.

The domes of Tuolomne are randomly spaced, often miles apart, but the ones we climbed on were never more than a half-hour hike along thin dirt-packed climber-worn paths from the road. The climbs blur in my memory, all a thin balancing act on holds that became smaller, then disappeared, mere dents of hope on vertical faces. At times grace failed me, and I pawed for holds, or my feet shuffled like I was wearing flip-flops, desperately trying to stick. Our calf muscles bulged from standing on sliver-sized holds, the tips of our fingers roughened thick with calluses.

I have this image from that summer: Jonathan shirtless, his broad shoulders shimmering golden brown, cut-off jeans hung low on his slim hips. I'm on the ground or hanging from a belay anchor, my head tilted back as I carefully feed out rope, my eyes squinting into the high California sun. Jonathan's moves were a seamless dance, like water across rock, his footwork precise, the tips of his shoes landing on holds and sticking as if he had invented them. When protection thinned, he'd hesitate for a moment, barely a heart beat of indecision, before moving upward. Looking up the expanse of rock, Jonathan's long bowed legs spread wide, his arms an arc toward the sky, his red swami belt a dash of color amidst it all, it looked like he was holding up the cliff.

At every belay ledge, Jonathan removed his tight climbing shoes, lit a Marlboro and casually belayed me up, the rope looped around his waist. As I climbed, I had to pay attention, learned to see a wrinkle that meant balance or safety. I took in the silence of those domes, heard them breath. In those moments when the rock cradled my body or offered me holds my heart opened up, and what I felt wasn't joy but a pain like the subtle ache of my feet in tight climbing shoes.

Breathing gulps of the high mountain air, I pulled onto those tight belay ledges, and our bodies, warm from the sun, touched lightly.

By mid-afternoon we were done, our fingertips raw, our toes aching from the unnatural tightness of our EBs. We wore our climbing shoes so tight that my left foot went numb for a week. We hiked to Tenaya Lake, a small blue-green gem nestled in the high mountains. A thin strip of sand served as our beach. There we stretched out under pine trees, performed our most decadent move, the Tenaya Lake layback. Quick dips in the icy water made us gasp for air. Those short swims were our idea of a shower, since the expense of the real ones at the campground kept us on a once-a-week schedule. As we rested by the lake, we'd chew on carrots, lunch and mid-afternoon snack wrapped into one.

At first, our Spartan diet slowed us down, our morning sugar crashes translating to falls on hard climbs, or motivation sapped by early afternoon. Then without understanding cause and effect, I came to expect-then enjoy- the shock of a body desperate for food. The natural dizzy high of climbing all day without eating translated to weakness in my legs, but also a carefree giddiness. I associated that light-headed feeling with the satisfaction of a hard day of climbing. I came to equate hunger with happiness.

In the evenings we hiked back to our tent site. Rarely did we have fellow Tenters next door, but there was always someone downhill from us, usually an older couple who became curious about our gear, then asked the standard questions about climbing: how did we get the rope up there? Did we ever fall? I'd stop and tell them about the climbs we had done on Meriolomne Dome, Daff Dome, Pywiack Dome, Stately Pleasure Dome. I took in their puzzled looks and realized that the language I spoke-of smears and crimpers, run-outs and bombproof belays- hardly made sense to them.

Back at our campsite I'd tell Jonathan about my conversations. "Yep honey, should we eat more hotdogs now, or some hamburgers?" Jonathan asked. "Let's have both," I responded. "And then that three layer frosted cake." We laughed at our simple humor, but I knew if they offered me a burger I would snatch it up. And I also knew that their lives and ours were not- except for the food- so different. We depended on the next hold to keep us together while they were bound by the next grilled meal.

The one day we were caught in a storm, our neighbor waited at the window of her trailer, watching for us. I thanked her once, twice and then again the next morning. "What would she have done, come out and rescued us?" Jonathan asked. And he was right, but her concern, housed securely in the shelter of her trailer felt real, and good. I wanted someone to care about my safety, about the dangers my body encountered; I wanted someone to care that I was getting thin.

Dinners varied little from noodles with tomato sauce. We'd sit over our hissing campstove taking in the smell of the pine trees that ringed our campsite, or the steaks cooking over an open fire. The early night sky, bluing into black, shed enough light for us to cook and write in our journals. The silence surrounding us was interrupted only by the hum of a camp generator at work. Soon after darkness settled in, we crawled into our tent. The ripe dampness of sleeping bags and salty bodies filled that small space, made us marvel at our own stink. "Things are mighty odorous around here," was Jonathan's goodnight line. I always laughed. That smell grew out of hard climbs, where our passion was spent; it rarely invited anything beyond a good night kiss.

What had begun in Vedauwoo continued through the summer. I remember making love once after showers and a six-pack of beer. For a while I told myself we didn't make love because we were so dirty. Then I said we needed a six-pack to lubricate our love. But down deep I sensed neither beer nor showers were a solution. I didn't search out an answer, didn't try to locate the thread that might connect us. Perhaps I sensed it didn't exist. What was important was that we climbed well together, our connection on the rock intuitive and bound by an eleven-millimeter rope.

Jonathan and I only had one fight that summer. What began in specifics- me wanting to lead a climb- led to a larger discussion about selfishness and generosity. I argued with the passion of youth that people could be genuinely selfless, generous, that I belayed Jonathan for him. All those hours, beginning with Penis Dimension in Vedauwoo that I held his rope, cheered him on were only because I wanted him to get up those routes. Jonathan was clear that generosity was outside the range of human nature: I belayed him because I wanted to get up the route, was doing it for myself. I knew that Jonathan was Republican to my Democrat, and had long forsaken talking politics. But this was bigger than politics and ideals. This was my life. I had belayed him not because I wanted to get up the route, but because I wanted him to love me.

"Do you really believe that people can't be generous?" I asked over and over. What I was saying was: do you really believe that people can't love? He shook his head no. Nothing in his life could confirm that. He'd been screwed over again and again by family and luck, by jobs and love.

"Why should I trust anyone?" he asked.

I sat back. Climbing is based on the trust held between partners.

I then understood why he so seldom fell, why he held on as if to life itself through desperate moves. He didn't assume that anyone was belaying him attentively, would catch him if he fell. He couldn't see that I was his girlfriend that I would catch him, if he just let me.

Fueled by a six-pack, our argument traveled in maddening circles. As I crawled into my sleeping bag the bitterness of the beer lingered in my mouth.

At five the next morning, pots and pans clanged onto the ground. I peered out of the tent and there, not more than ten feet from me hunched a black bear, using its dexterous front paws to get at the noodles that remained at the bottom of the pot. In the heat of our argument the night before, I had forgotten to wash our dishes. The deep musky warmth of the bear greeted me as I stared at its shiny black muzzle. Before I could move, our neighbors knocked pans together, and the bear ran off, its hind legs kicking high as he disappeared into the woods.

"That was cool," Jonathan said, peering out of the tent.

"Yeh." And our fight was forgotten.

***

It was a perfect summer: terrific hard climbs, one bear easily scared off, only one fight. In my journal I brag about the routes that we did, and often my thoughts turned toward how idyllic our situation was, a script for an adventure-filled romance. In calmer moments, I wrote of living in the present, of treasuring each day knowing that it couldn't last.

Nothing bad happened. So how did I end up ninety pounds light? What I couldn't write, my body spoke for me. And, it was telling secrets: I am lonely, it said. I am fragile. I don't like myself. I felt exposed. As a climber, I live for the feeling of exposure, that sudden dropping away of the cliff that leaves the heart and mind dizzy. But this dizziness only made me nauseous.

All summer, my body had been making noises. Each time, I ignored the pleas, for attention. Two sequences from the video of my mind remain vivid.

One: Two days before we were to leave on this trip, I stood in the Planned Parenthood office in downtown Boulder. My pregnancy test read positive, the nurse said calmly. I stared at the brown shag carpeting, then at the brown wood paneling that looked the color of dried blood. What the nurse said sunk in slowly because it didn't make sense. Jonathan and I had made love only that one time, our pre-trip commitment. The absurdity of my situation- one night of sex and I was pregnant- made me howl, made me believe there was a God: a righteous punishing one.

Nothing was going to get in the way of this trip. I scheduled an abortion for the morning, and we would leave for Tuolomne in the afternoon. I cried, wrote a long letter to my sister, hated my body for the way it had done me wrong at a time when I needed it to be strong, light, ready to follow Jonathan up climbs.

I bicycled alone the twelve long miles along a four-lane highway into Boulder. Three kind nurses hovered around as a doctor performed the initial physical. "How pregnant are you?" she asked, pressing deep into my gut, her hands exploring my insides that felt disconnected from the rest of my body. I knew to the day, perhaps to the minute how pregnant I should be. She shook her head and said, 'No, you're the size of a pea." With one hand she made a circle, thumb and forefinger curling around each other. I leapt off the table, grabbed my clothes and ran from that office. The next day my period started. That was the last time I bled for the next four years.

Two: I stopped on the dusty trail leading into the climb and pulled down my green shorts, squatted to pee. Ten minutes later, at the base of the route, Jonathan organized his gear while I dropped the rope in a coiled heap, then stepped away a few paces. I peed again. Mid-way up the route I called up to Jonathan, sixty feet above me. "Can't you wait?" he called down. Through the clear high air I could hear him as if we were speaking across the picnic table. "No," I said quietly. He held the thick yellow rope tight, and I squirmed, pulling down my pants. A small trickle ran down the smooth rock, instantly evaporating in the high hot sun.

In the public showers later that night I scrubbed between my legs, imagined that I could wash away whatever was wrong.

"What's the matter with you?" Jonathan asked.

I shrugged, wishing whatever it was would go away. A few days later yellow turned to red. I couldn't ignore that, or the spasms in my gut. Reluctantly, we packed a small backpack and hitchhiked out of the park, into civilization: Carson City, Nevada.

"We have enough money for a motel, I said, counting our stash that we kept rolled up inside my pack.

Jonathan had other plans. I followed him as he ambled into one of the many local gambling halls. He headed straight for the craps table. We'd had luck there on our trip out, winning small amounts of money to pay for breakfast or lunch.

Jonathan stood next to the other men, placed his bets with confidence and took his earnings in stride. I stood behind him, staring as he placed his chips beneath a bright wide light that hung like a cap over the table. After the dice were flung from one end of the green table to the other, he cheered or cursed quietly. I looked around the table. I wasn't the only woman standing in the shadows, squeezing her man's hand while he sweated and focused on his luck. But those women wore small tight dresses and had blond hair that swept back from their foreheads. My jeans hung from my hips, and my hair was stiff from sun and wind. The urge to pee made me fidget. While a cocktail waitress handed Jonathan another beer, he slipped me a wad of wrinkled bills. Thrilled, I counted. One hundred. Then I held my breath as I slowly handed back his winnings: ninety, eighty, seventy, sixty. When it got to thirty I took him by the arm, could tell by the slack in his body that he had had enough beer. I hauled him away from the table, desperate to check into a motel. "I could have won more," he insisted as we walked out into the bright flashing lights of the city. "Thirty dollars is all we need," I explained again.

Actually, we only needed $19.90 and a few more dollars to buy a frozen cheesecake, which we ate until ill. I spent the night on the white porcelain toilet seat, bleeding and crying. I wondered if I should call my parents to tell them the end was near.

"You're not dying," Jonathan said.

The next morning at the hospital the nurse gave me some pills, patted me on the shoulder and said, "Next time this happens, honey, drink cranberry juice." It was a girl thing and there in the hospital I wanted to trade in my body, for the non-girl kind.

We hitchhiked back to the Meadows, were climbing again by late afternoon. "You ok now?" Jonathan asked as I dangled from a belay, one hundred feet off the ground. I nodded. "Sorry."

That summer, my body hurt. But that's what it meant to be a climber: your feet hurt, your fingertips tore. Some parts bled others stopped bleeding. It was a sign of my love, my devotion to it all. The point was to climb through the pain.

Finally, it was too much and we left Tuolomne when we could climb no more, when our fingertips had all split and were bleeding, when our feet ached even in sneakers, when we were weary of staring into the sun. All our rides home were enchanted and a trucker left us off not more than two blocks from Jonathan's home in Boulder.

School started two weeks later. I had responsibilities as a resident advisor, counseling twenty freshmen girls. I took my job seriously, stayed up until three in the morning listening to their "horrible boyfriend stories." Focusing on their problems helped me dodge questions from friends. "What happened to you?" "Are you ok?" "Let's get something to eat sometime." "Are you eating?" Of course I was eating, I laughed. But when I stood on the scale at the gym the dial swung to ninety pounds. The questions and the scale said one thing, but when I looked in the mirror I couldn't see how that matched the facts, the concern. There I was- Susan- only with a new short summer hair cut.

On the one hand, a focus so keen I could see a ripple on a wall of rock as a hold, on the other a blindness that could not see the collar bones that protruded, or the fact that the thighs were solid, yes, but only with a ribbon of muscle.

Being thin was good: I could do more pull-ups; I could do harder climbs. Being thin was good: I loved Jonathan; I loved climbing.

Girl. Girlfriend. Climber girl. I've spent the past eighteen years appalled by her laughter and doubts, her romantic notions of love.

She was so normal in her desires for love, from him, from the rock. She was utterly ordinary in the way she slipped into thinness. Now, when I see girls like her, shadows, literally, of the younger me, I think: you are brave. I want to tell them: what we love most can destroy us. But they won't listen; I wouldn't have. I would have said: you don't know what it's like to hurt this much.

Climber girl. She wanted the next hold but she wanted her idea of love more. That almost killed her. Not a long fall, but the falling into herself, her sadness, her loneliness, her hunger.

I have to try and tell her story, not the perfect climbing summer story but the inner story, as complicated and ordinary as it is. And I promise to tell her story without embarrassment. In the telling is forgiveness.

Questions for Reflection

1. How do you think this author "slipped into thinness?"

2. How might her experience have been similar to those of other outdoor adventurers and athletes?

3. What do you think might be critical components of an outdoor adventure education and/or therapy program for women and girls with body image and eating disorders?

4. If you could say something meaningful to that young "Climber Girl" or perhaps to the young girl *you* used to be, what might you say?

Contributors

Allison Bradley, Ph.D. has worked with women in a variety of roles since 1989 focusing on domestic violence and adventure programming. Dr. Bradley designs and facilitates "community initiatives" and training programs around domestic violence, emotional intelligence, and other topics through Crossroads Collaboratives. She is currently authoring a curriculum for the development of community based domestic violence strategies. Dr. Bradley lives in Kalamazoo, Michigan with her husband Scott, son Garret and Dalmatian Zoe; she is attempting to learn to play the cello in her spare time.

Sylvia Cole, LCSW-C is an Employee Assistance Counselor for American Psych Systems of Bethesda, Maryland and a sometimes writer/poet who has aspired to enter adventure therapy with groups since joining the Association for Experiential Education (AEE) in 1997. She is also affiliated with the Lesbian, Gay, Bi-Sexual and Allies professional group in AEE. Sylvia was a camp counselor in Pennsylvania from 1980-1985, and she went on to study psychology and religion. While working as a landscaper in the Washington, D.C. area, she did social work internships with persons living with AIDS, gays and lesbians in early addictions recovery, and survivors of sexual assault though the Whitman-Walker Clinic and the D.C. Rape Crisis Center.

Jean Faulk has a diverse background as a homemaker, executive secretary, and business owner. Along with her husband, Joe, and son, Brian, she founded Canoe Escape, Inc. in 1991. Canoe Escape is a canoe/kayak rental and retail business in Tampa, Florida. The business is a natural for Jean as it combines her love of nature and the outdoors and her interest in the conservation and preservation of the "special places" in our own backyards with an opportunity to educate and serve others about the joy of rediscovering and reconnecting with the planet through outdoor activities. Jean feels that while many people are born with a gift for writing or discover their "voice" along the way for herself, she has discovered what she calls the "declaratory statement." After an experience that resonates in her being she can't help but declare "There should be a poem for this!" At some later time, a few hours, a week, a year, the words start to arrive. Actually putting "by Jean Faulk" beneath the poem's name seemed incorrect. She interprets this to mean "by the hand of" Jean Faulk.

Karla Henderson, Ph.D., CLP is Professor and Chair of the Department of Recreation and Leisure Studies at the University of North Carolina at Chapel Hill. She loves the outdoors but has tended to write about it more than participate in activities. That problem is being resolved as she focuses on "walking the talk" so she can be a more enlightened writer. Her areas of research are women and gender related to leisure and the outdoors and on research and evaluation methods.

Jackie Kiewa works as a lecturer in Outdoor Education and Leisure Studies at Griffith University in Brisbane, Australia. She has been a keen climber and paddler for twenty years or so, combining these activities with her work and her family of three children. She has paddled and climbed in Australia, New Zealand, the United States, and the central Asian countries of Uzbekistan and Kyrgistan. Now forty-five years of age, she sees no reason to slow down, but is looking forward to many more years of active life.

T.A. Loeffler, Ph.D. is an avid outdoor adventurer and ice hockey player who teaches recreation and outdoor education at Memorial University of Newfoundland. After graduating from the University of Minnesota with a doctorate in Recreation, Park and Leisure Studies,

T.A. has pursued research in women's competency development in experiential education, the portrayal of women in the outdoor media, women's career development in outdoor leadership, and the influence of outdoor program philosophy on program delivery. T.A.'s recent publications include two chapters in *Women's Voices in Experiential Education* and an article for *The Journal of Experiential Education* which explores competency in both professional and personal voices.

Mary McClintock provides research, writing and editing services through her business, Better-Me-Than-You Research and Editorial Services. Her passions include sea kayaking, whitewater canoeing, contra dancing, and spending time outdoors with other lesbians. She lives in Conway, MA. Her publications include articles in *Camping Magazine*, *The Journal of Experiential Education*, *Atlantic Coastal Kayaker*, *Women's Voices in Experiential Education* (Karen Warren, Ed.), and *Teaching for Diversity and Social Justice: A Sourcebook* (Adams, Bell, and Griffin, Eds.).

Diane McManus describes herself as a "poet in motion." She is an editor, writer, runner, dark-chocolate eater, and cat lover. Currently Managing Editor of the *Journal of Modern Literature*, she has taught writing courses at Temple, Drexel, and West Chester Universities and has presented writing and journal-keeping workshops at conferences. As a runner, she has "more love for the game than talent for it," and is still in pursuit of a younger, faster self she met several years ago (pre-injuries). She has completed five marathons, including Boston, although she now prefers shorter distances. "Running is a way of breaking free and playing, recapturing the child in me, noticing my world more. So it only follows that poems result." *Here you begin* is her first collection of poems; she has previously published poetry and fiction in *Runner's Gazette*.

Molly Benson Prince has taught social studies for five and half years at Columbus Academy in Columbus, OH. For the past two and half years she has also served as School Director of Student Life. Her summertime adventures have included working for the Rocky Mountain Branch of N.O.L.S., North Carolina Outward Bound, and the Adventure Education Center in Worthington, OH. Molly received her Master's in Experiential Education from Mankato State University.

Nina S. Roberts, M.A., completed her Master's degree in Outdoor Recreation and Resource Management from the University of Maryland at College Park and is currently pursuing a Ph.D. in Recreation Resources at Colorado State University. Nina is the former Assistant Director of the Conservation Career Development Program of the Student Conservation Association (SCA) providing outdoor education programs and career services for primarily people of color and women. She currently works for SCA part-time as a Research Associate while engaged in doctoral studies at CSU. She is the former Chairperson of the Publications Advisory Committee and Women's Professional Group Representative to the Board of Directors for the Association for Experiential Education. Nina is also involved as a consultant with the AEE/NAALA Professional Group (Natives, Africans, Asians, Latinos and Allies), and Girls Outdoors, Inc. in Fort Collins, Colorado. Her research interests include recreation land management, wilderness studies, outdoor programming and leadership, youth development, adventure education, environmental education, gender issues, and race and culture. Her work has been published in numerous scholarly journals as well as books and magazines. As a bi-racial woman, Nina's research has guided her to write about women of diverse ethnic and cultural backgrounds, and explore their connection to leisure activities in the natural environment. She has presented her work at conferences regionally and nationally, as well as in Southeast Asia.

Susan Fox-Rogers is the editor of nine anthologies including *Solo: On Her Own Adventure, Two in the Wild: Tales of Adventure from Friends, Mothers and Daughters,* and *Another Wilderness: New Outdoor Writing by Women.* She has an MFA from the University of Arizona and lives in Tucson.

Anne Vilen is an avid hiker and backpacker living in the mountains of North Carolina with her husband and two young children. She makes her living teaching creative writing and writing therapy in community and health care settings. Her essays and poems have appeared in numerous commercial and literary magazines including *New Moon Parenting, On The Issues, Common Boundary, Iowa Woman,* and *High Plains Literary Review.*

Donna Glee Williams is a registered nurse with experience in pediatric, psychiatric, stress management and addictions nursing. She also has a M.F.A. in writing and a Ph.D. in English. She left hospital nursing and college teaching to work as an experiential educator at the North Carolina Center for the Advancement of Teaching, where she plans and leads learning adventures for the spiritual revitalization of North Carolina public school teachers.

About the Editor

Lisa West-Smith, Ph.D., LCSW is a psychotherapist and educator who has worked in the field of eating disorders for over a decade. In addition to working with individuals and groups in clinical practice, Lisa has developed and taught special topics psychology & women's studies courses on *Women & Nature* and *Body Image, Eating Problems & Cultural Contexts* for the University of Cincinnati. She has presented educational workshops on eating disorders interventions all across the US for organizations including: St. Luke Hospital; Aurora University; Christ Hospital; the Association for Experiential Education; the National Board of Certified Counselors; the State Board of Social Work of Kentucky; and the Ohio Counselor and Social Worker Board. Lisa is an avid outdoorswoman and recreational athlete who enjoys canoeing, kayaking, hiking and running through the woods. She and her long time husband Mickey are currently building a new home atop a wild rose covered ridge in the foothills of Northern Kentucky. They are the proud parents of three beautiful daughters. Lisa can be reached at the Adventurehaven Center for Eating Disorders Education and Recovery in Edgewood, KY at lisa@adventurehaven.com.